GRAPHIC LIBRARY™

INVENTIONS AND DISCOVERY

ALEXANDER GRAHAM BELL AND THE TELEPHONE

by Jennifer Fandel

illustrated by Keith Tucker

Consultant:
Michael E. Gorman
Professor of Science, Technology, and Society
University of Virginia
Charlottesville, Virginia

Capstone press®

Mankato, Minnesota

Graphic Library is published by Capstone Press,
1710 Roe Crest Drive, North Mankato, Minnesota 56003.
www.capstonepub.com

Library of Congress Cataloging-in-Publication Data
Fandel, Jennifer.
Alexander Graham Bell and the telephone / by Jennifer Fandel; illustrated by Keith Tucker.
p. cm.— (Graphic library. Inventions and discovery)
Summary: "In graphic novel format, tells the story of how Alexander Graham Bell came up with the telephone, and how his invention changed the way people communicate"—Provided by publisher.
Includes bibliographical references and index.
ISBN: 978-0-7368-6478-7 (hardcover)
ISBN: 978-0-7368-9640-5 (softcover pbk.)
1. Bell, Alexander Graham, 1847–1922—Juvenile literature. 2. Inventors—United States—Biography—Juvenile literature. 3. Telephone—History—Juvenile literature. I. Tucker, Keith. II. Title. III. Series.
TK6143.B4F36 2007
621.385092—dc22 2006004082

Designers
Jason Knudson and Kim Brown

Colorist
Sarah Trover

Editor
Christine Peterson

Editor's note: Direct quotations from primary sources are indicated by a yellow background.

Direct quotations appear on the following pages:
Pages 14–15, from the notebooks of Alexander Graham Bell; page 17, from a 1915 speech by Thomas Watson; page 20, from a letter written by Alexander Graham Bell to his father; part of the Alexander Graham Bell Family Papers at the Library of Congress (http:/memory.loc.gov/ammem/bellhtml/bellhome.html).
Pages 24 and 25, from Bell's account of the transcontinental phone call as published in *Alexander Graham Bell: The Life and Times of the Man Who Invented the Telephone* by Edwin S. Grosvenor and Morgan Wesson (New York: Harry Abrams, 1997).

Printed in the United States 5619

TABLE OF CONTENTS

CHAPTER 1

MESSAGES AND SOUND

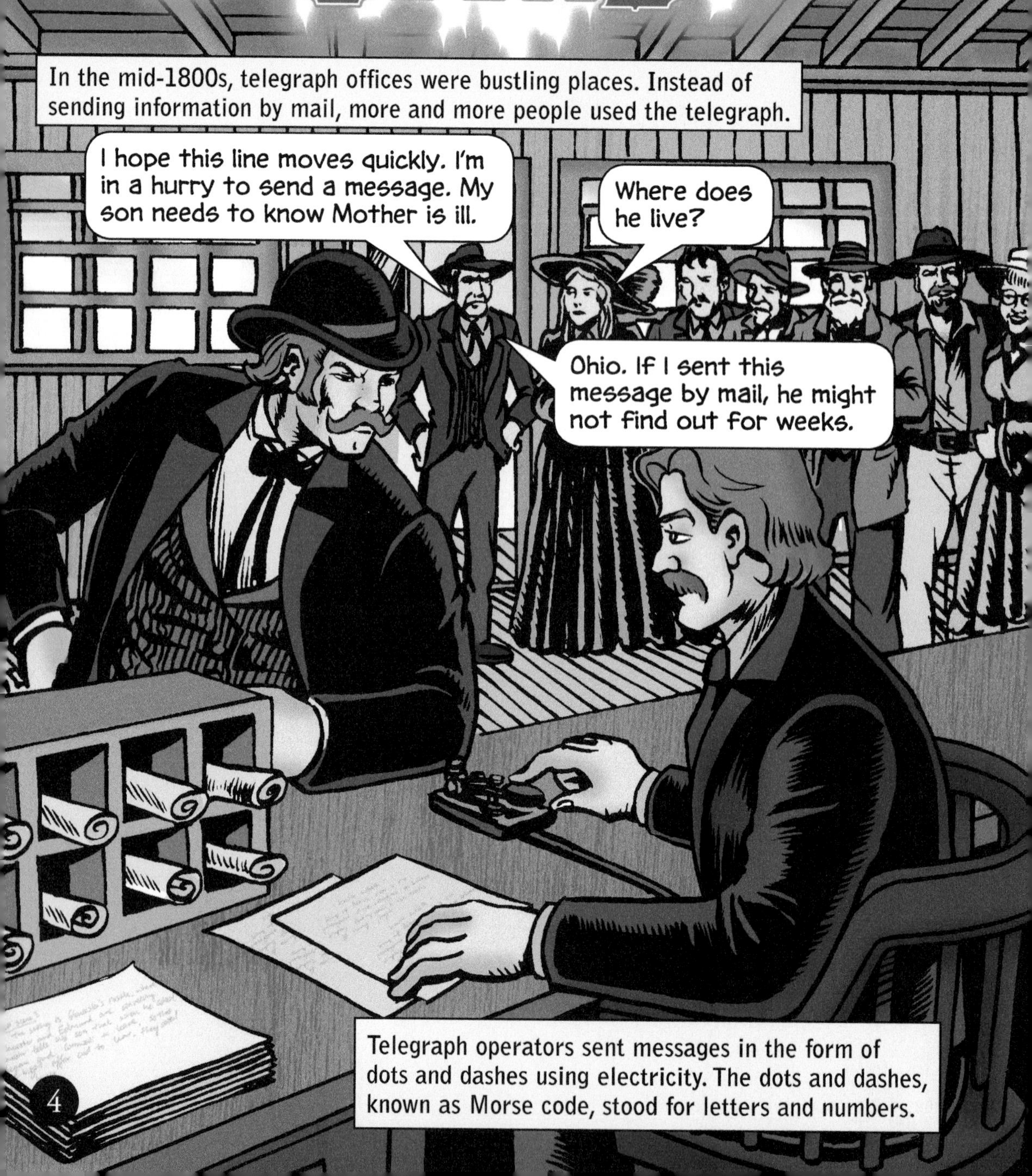
In the mid-1800s, telegraph offices were bustling places. Instead of sending information by mail, more and more people used the telegraph.
I hope this line moves quickly. I'm in a hurry to send a message. My son needs to know Mother is ill.
Where does he live?
Ohio. If I sent this message by mail, he might not find out for weeks.
Telegraph operators sent messages in the form of dots and dashes using electricity. The dots and dashes, known as Morse code, stood for letters and numbers.

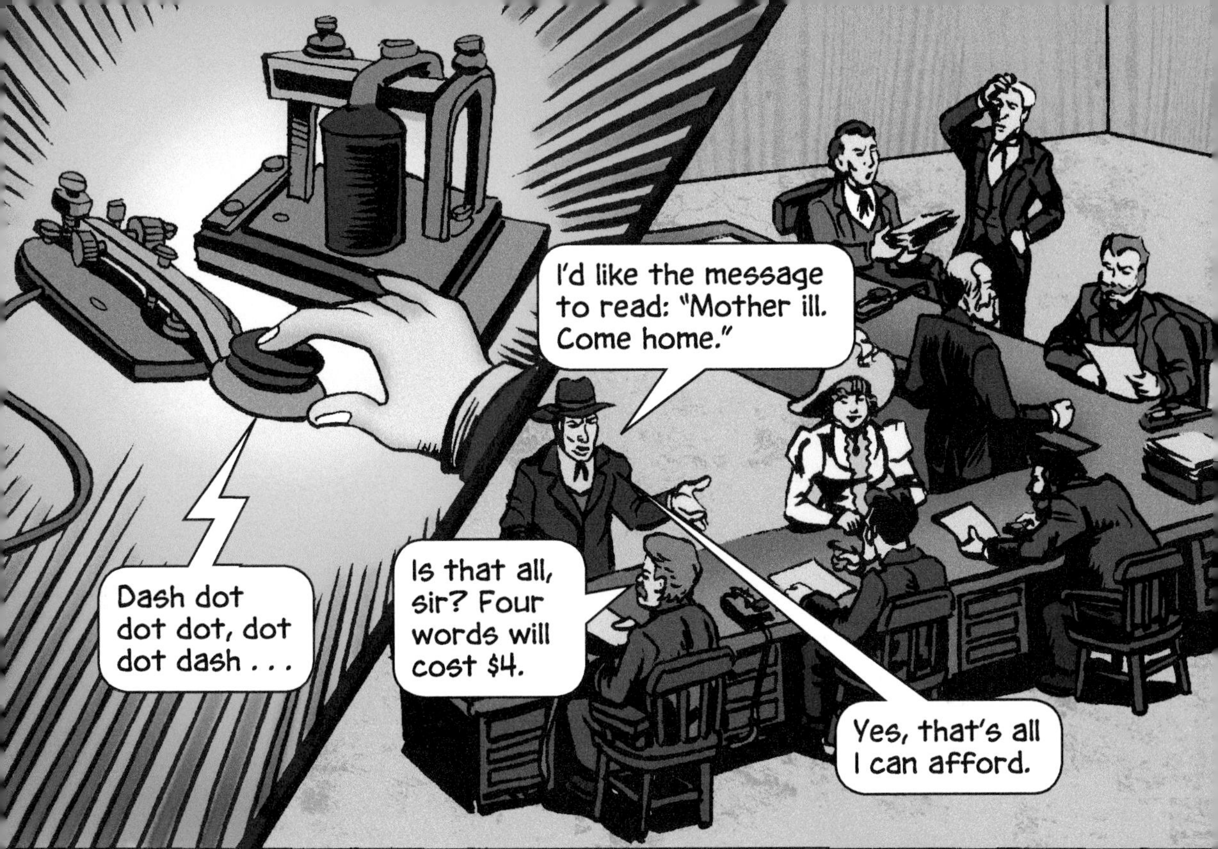
I'd like the message to read: "Mother ill. Come home."
Is that all, sir? Four words will cost $4.
Yes, that's all I can afford.
Dash dot dot dot, dot dot dash . . .

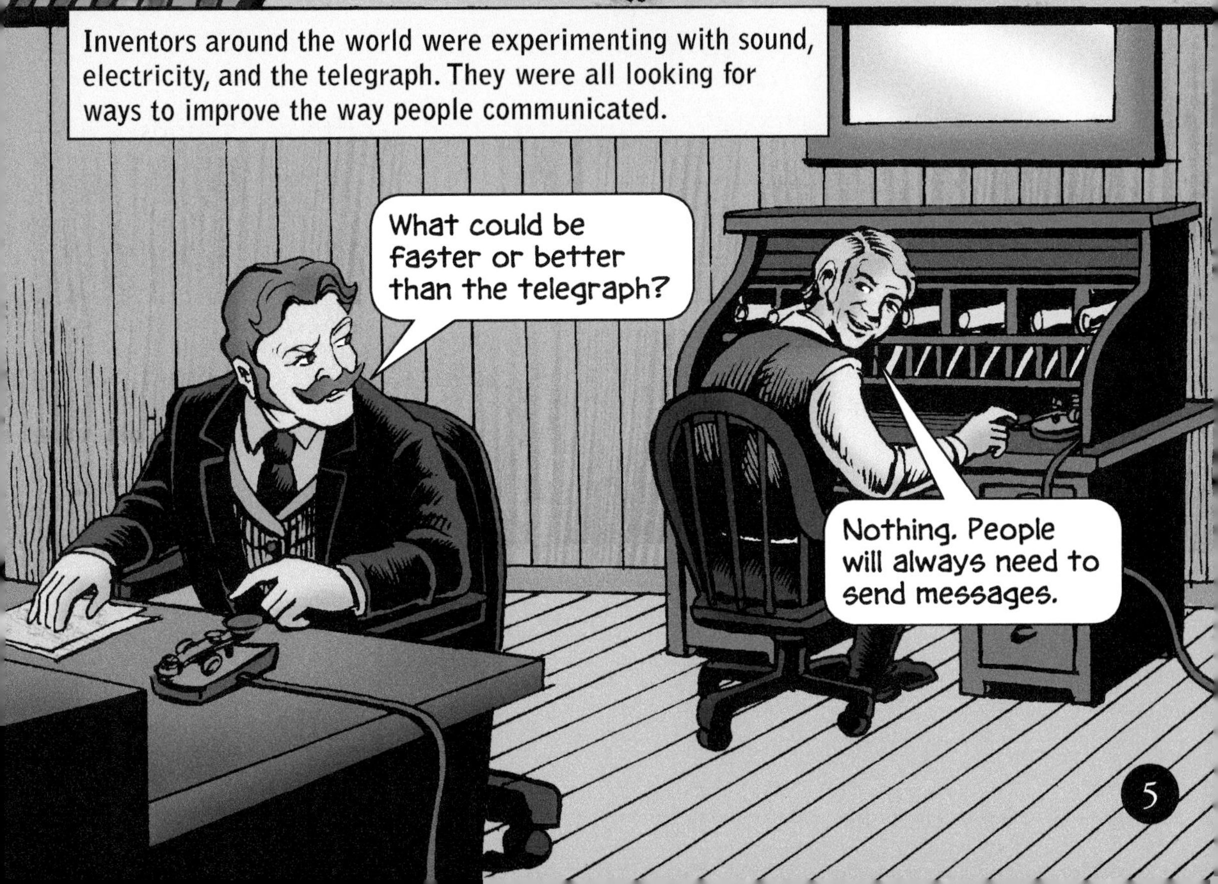
Inventors around the world were experimenting with sound, electricity, and the telegraph. They were all looking for ways to improve the way people communicated.
What could be faster or better than the telegraph?
Nothing. People will always need to send messages.

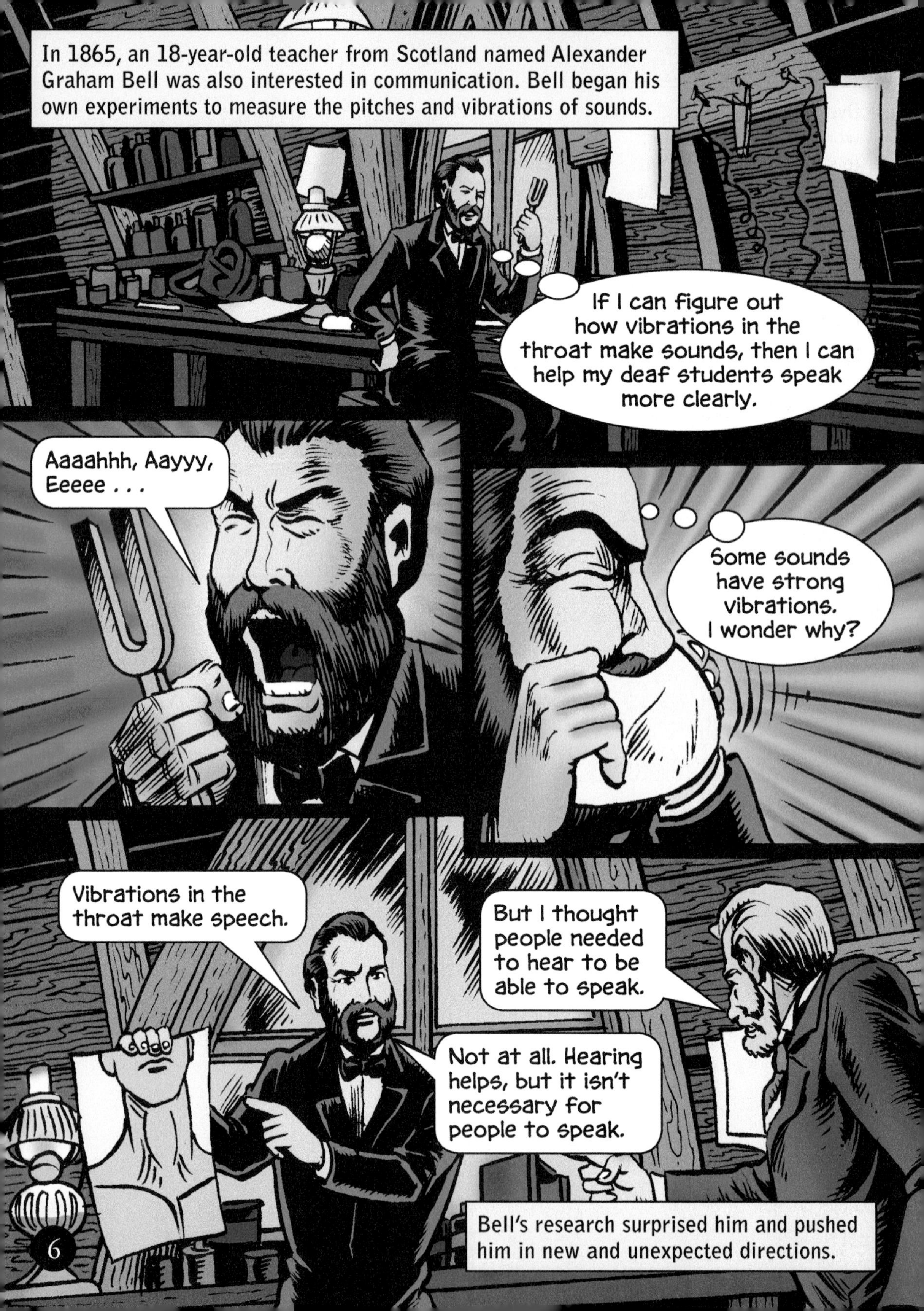
In 1865, an 18-year-old teacher from Scotland named Alexander Graham Bell was also interested in communication. Bell began his own experiments to measure the pitches and vibrations of sounds.
If I can figure out how vibrations in the throat make sounds, then I can help my deaf students speak more clearly.
Aaaahhh, Aayyy, Eeeee . . .
Some sounds have strong vibrations. I wonder why?
Vibrations in the throat make speech.
But I thought people needed to hear to be able to speak.
Not at all. Hearing helps, but it isn't necessary for people to speak.
Bell's research surprised him and pushed him in new and unexpected directions.

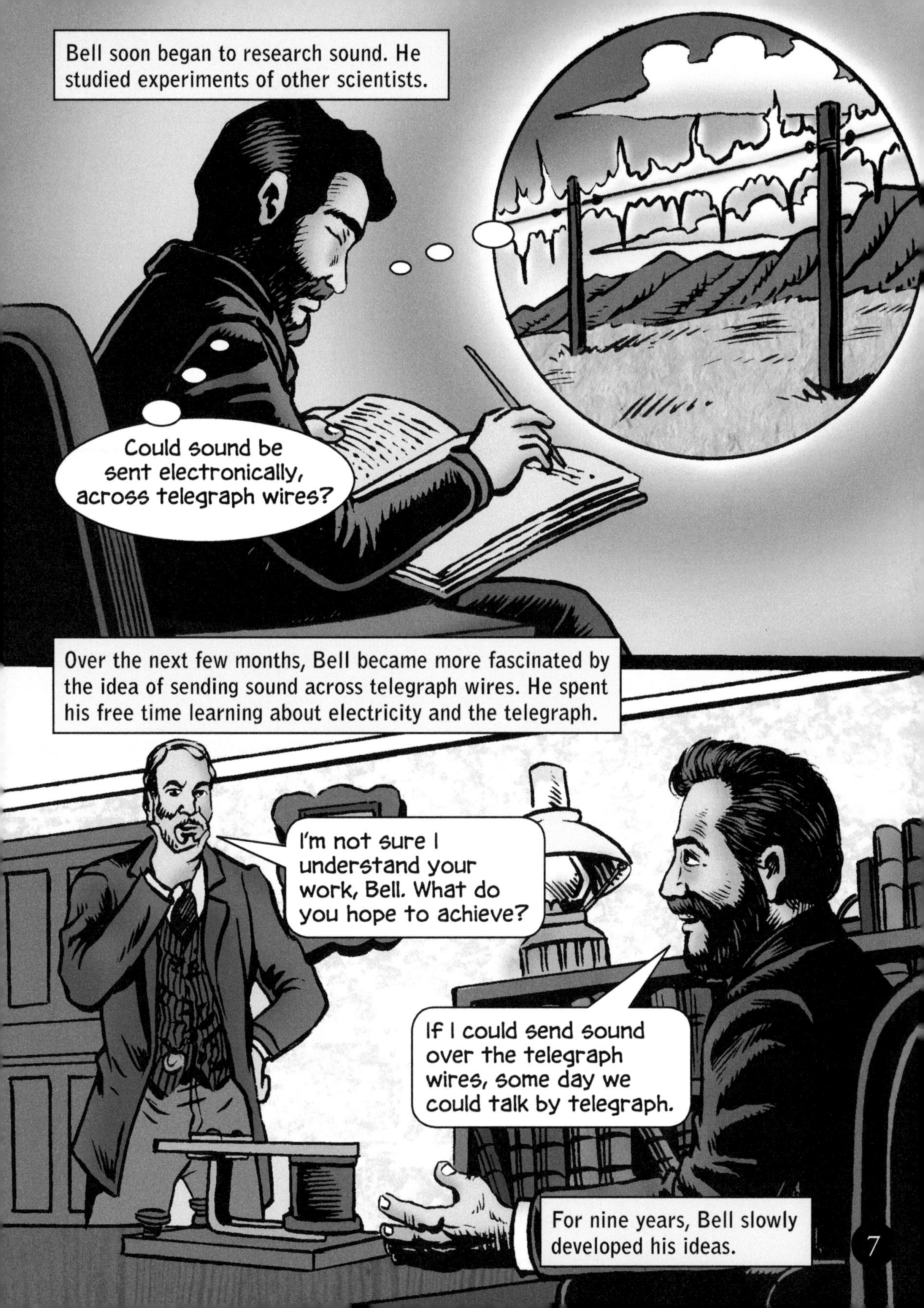
Bell soon began to research sound. He studied experiments of other scientists.
Could sound be sent electronically, across telegraph wires?
Over the next few months, Bell became more fascinated by the idea of sending sound across telegraph wires. He spent his free time learning about electricity and the telegraph.
I'm not sure I understand your work, Bell. What do you hope to achieve?
If I could send sound over the telegraph wires, some day we could talk by telegraph.
For nine years, Bell slowly developed his ideas.

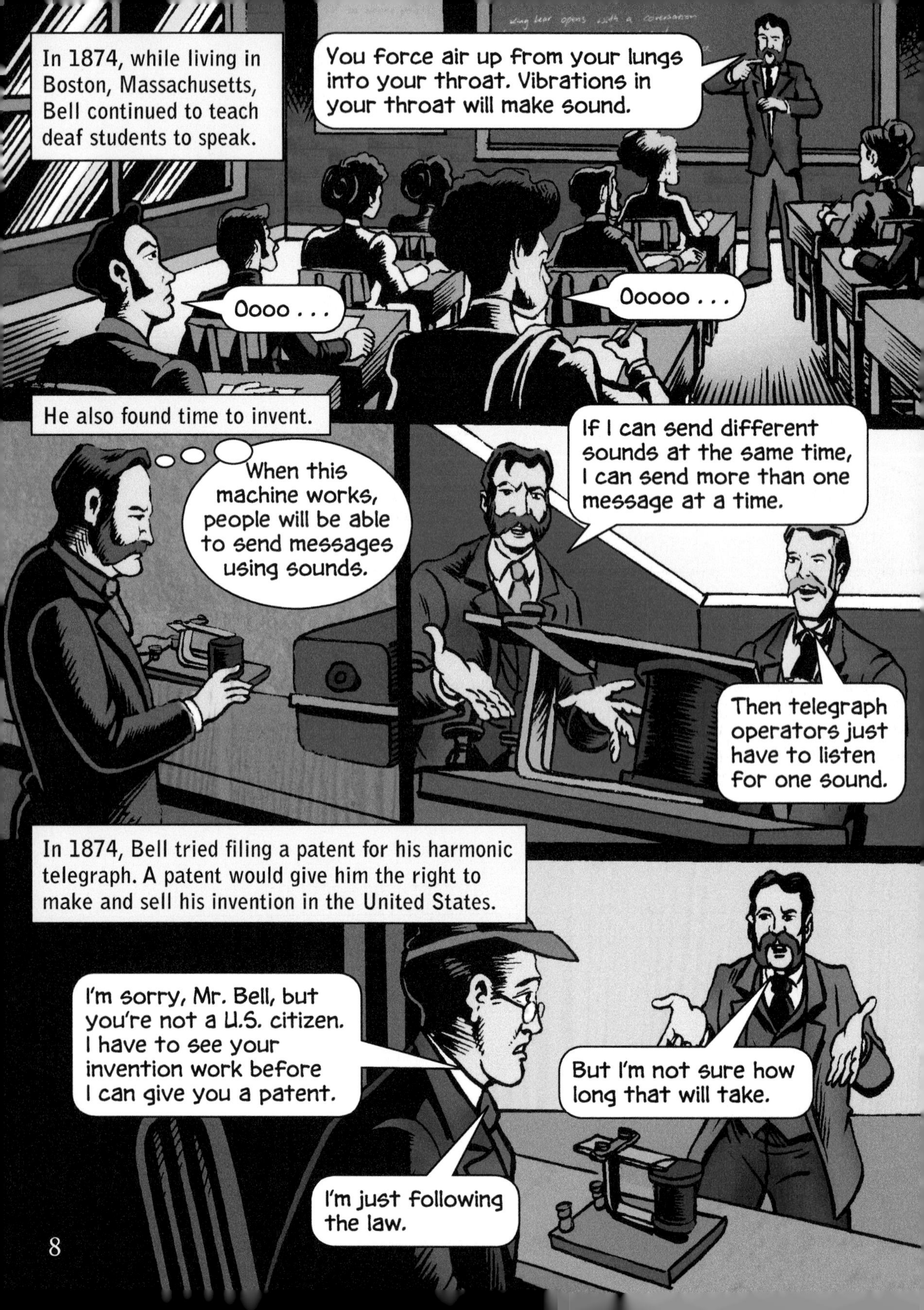
In 1874, while living in Boston, Massachusetts, Bell continued to teach deaf students to speak.
You force air up from your lungs into your throat. Vibrations in your throat will make sound.
Oooo . . .
Ooooo . . .
He also found time to invent.
When this machine works, people will be able to send messages using sounds.
If I can send different sounds at the same time, I can send more than one message at a time.
Then telegraph operators just have to listen for one sound.
In 1874, Bell tried filing a patent for his harmonic telegraph. A patent would give him the right to make and sell his invention in the United States.
I'm sorry, Mr. Bell, but you're not a U.S. citizen. I have to see your invention work before I can give you a patent.
But I'm not sure how long that will take.
I'm just following the law.

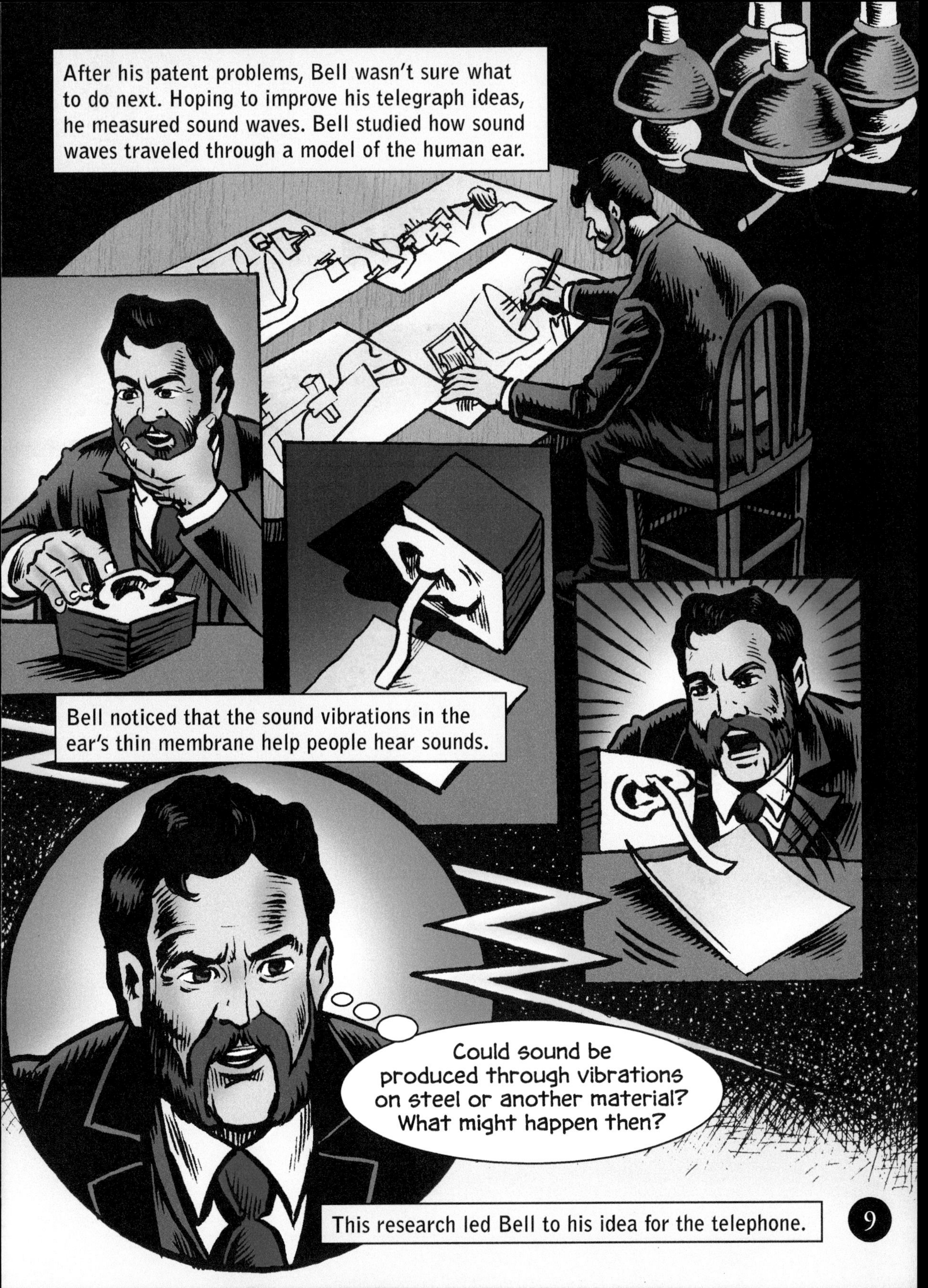
After his patent problems, Bell wasn't sure what to do next. Hoping to improve his telegraph ideas, he measured sound waves. Bell studied how sound waves traveled through a model of the human ear.
Bell noticed that the sound vibrations in the ear's thin membrane help people hear sounds.
Could sound be produced through vibrations on steel or another material? What might happen then?
This research led Bell to his idea for the telephone.

CHAPTER 2

AN AMAZING SOUND

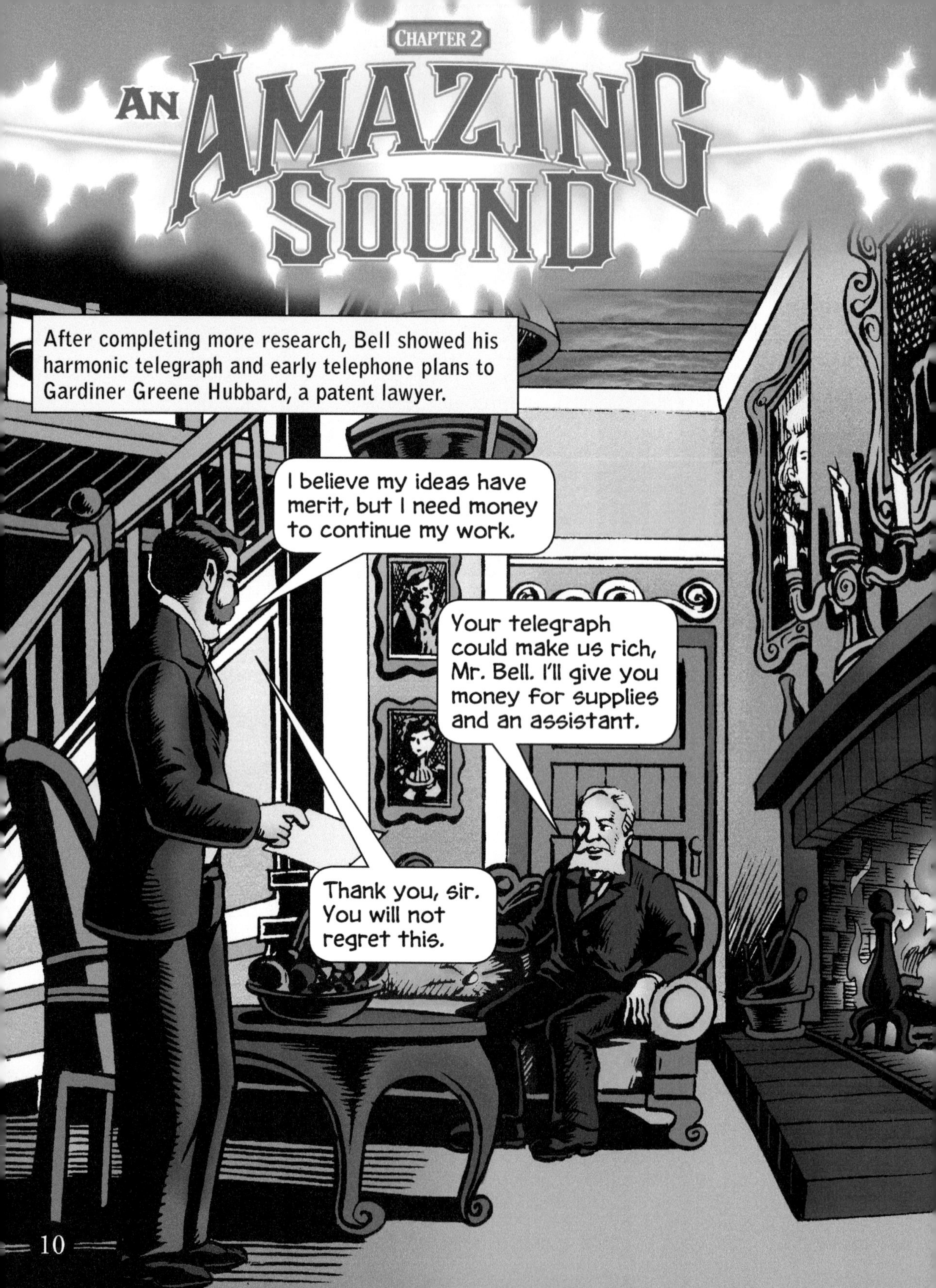
After completing more research, Bell showed his harmonic telegraph and early telephone plans to Gardiner Greene Hubbard, a patent lawyer.
I believe my ideas have merit, but I need money to continue my work.
Your telegraph could make us rich, Mr. Bell. I'll give you money for supplies and an assistant.
Thank you, sir. You will not regret this.

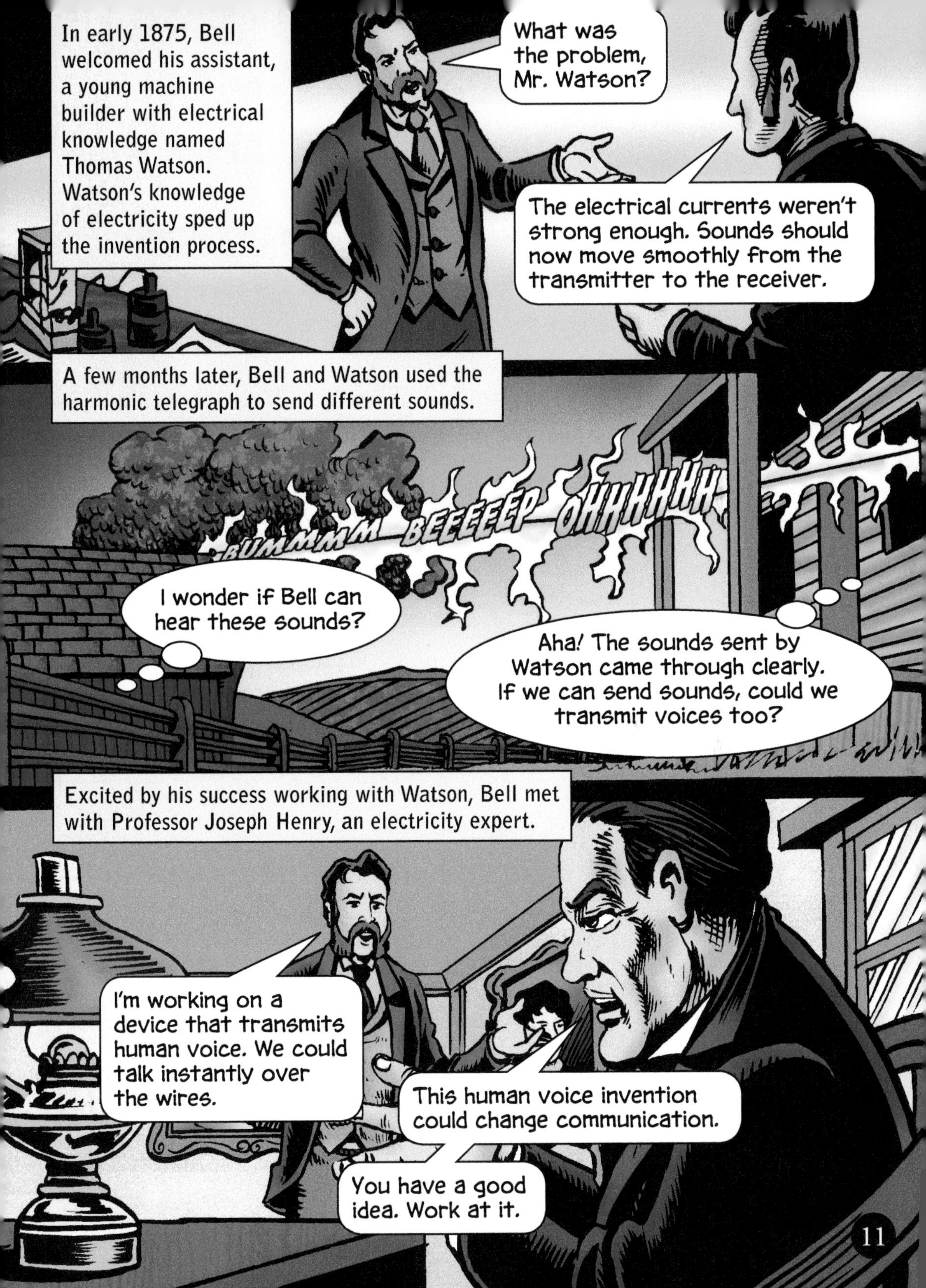
In early 1875, Bell welcomed his assistant, a young machine builder with electrical knowledge named Thomas Watson. Watson's knowledge of electricity sped up the invention process.
What was the problem, Mr. Watson?
The electrical currents weren't strong enough. Sounds should now move smoothly from the transmitter to the receiver.
A few months later, Bell and Watson used the harmonic telegraph to send different sounds.
BUMMMM BEEEEEP OHHHHHH
I wonder if Bell can hear these sounds?
Aha! The sounds sent by Watson came through clearly. If we can send sounds, could we transmit voices too?
Excited by his success working with Watson, Bell met with Professor Joseph Henry, an electricity expert.
I'm working on a device that transmits human voice. We could talk instantly over the wires.
This human voice invention could change communication.
You have a good idea. Work at it.

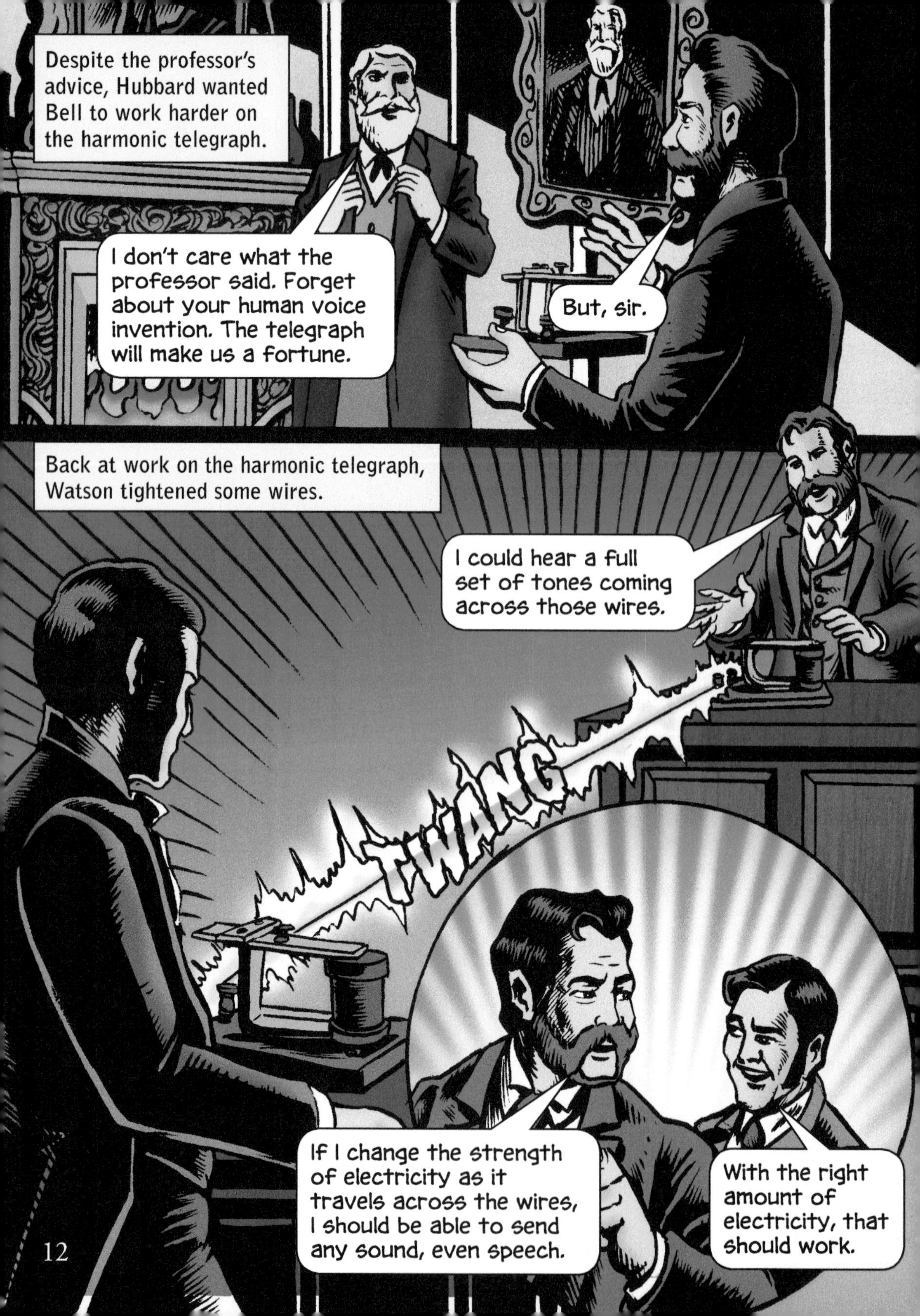
Despite the professor's advice, Hubbard wanted Bell to work harder on the harmonic telegraph.
I don't care what the professor said. Forget about your human voice invention. The telegraph will make us a fortune.
But, sir.
Back at work on the harmonic telegraph, Watson tightened some wires.
I could hear a full set of tones coming across those wires.
TWANG
If I change the strength of electricity as it travels across the wires, I should be able to send any sound, even speech.
With the right amount of electricity, that should work.

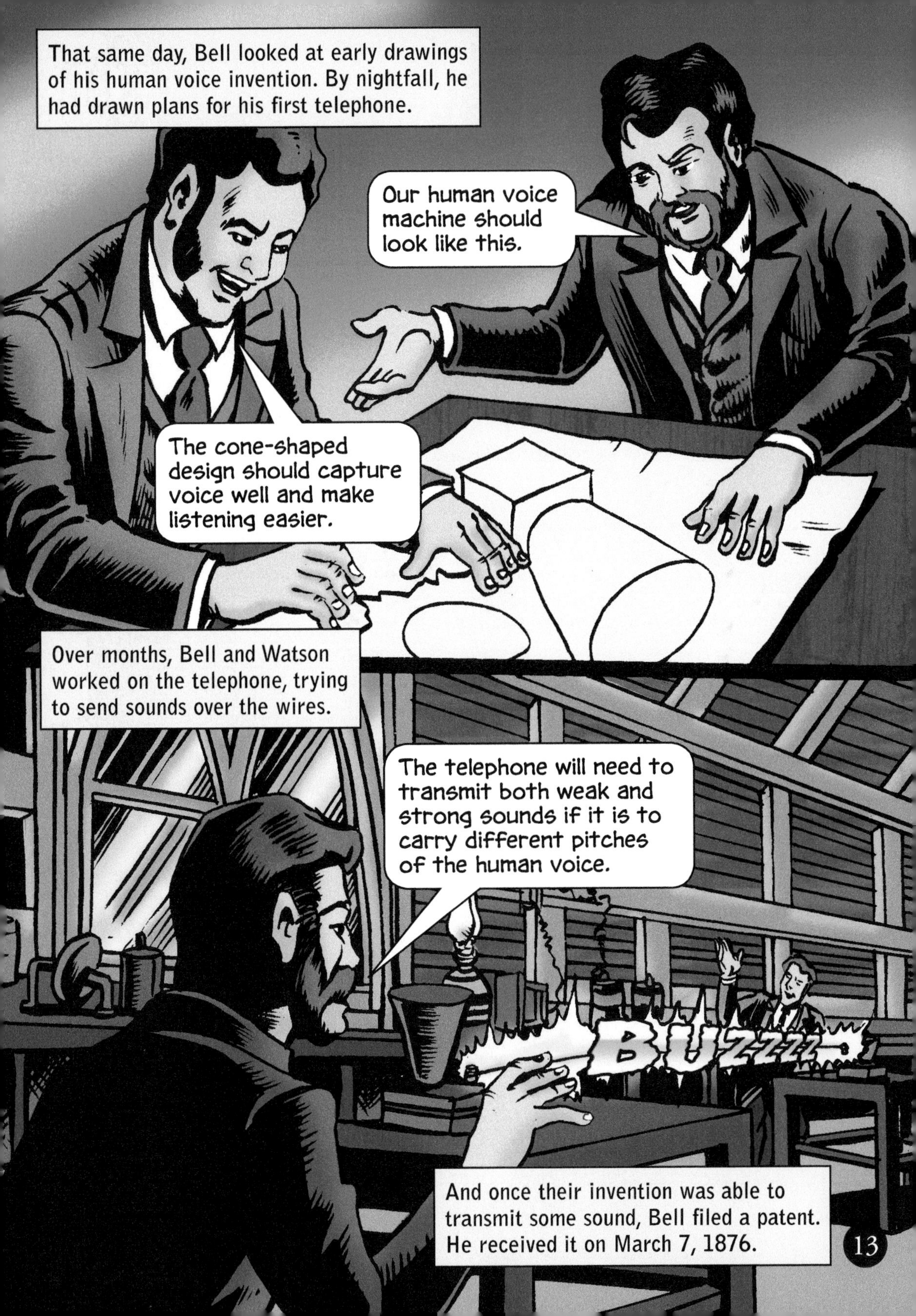
That same day, Bell looked at early drawings of his human voice invention. By nightfall, he had drawn plans for his first telephone.
Our human voice machine should look like this.
The cone-shaped design should capture voice well and make listening easier.
Over months, Bell and Watson worked on the telephone, trying to send sounds over the wires.
The telephone will need to transmit both weak and strong sounds if it is to carry different pitches of the human voice.
BUZZZZ
And once their invention was able to transmit some sound, Bell filed a patent. He received it on March 7, 1876.

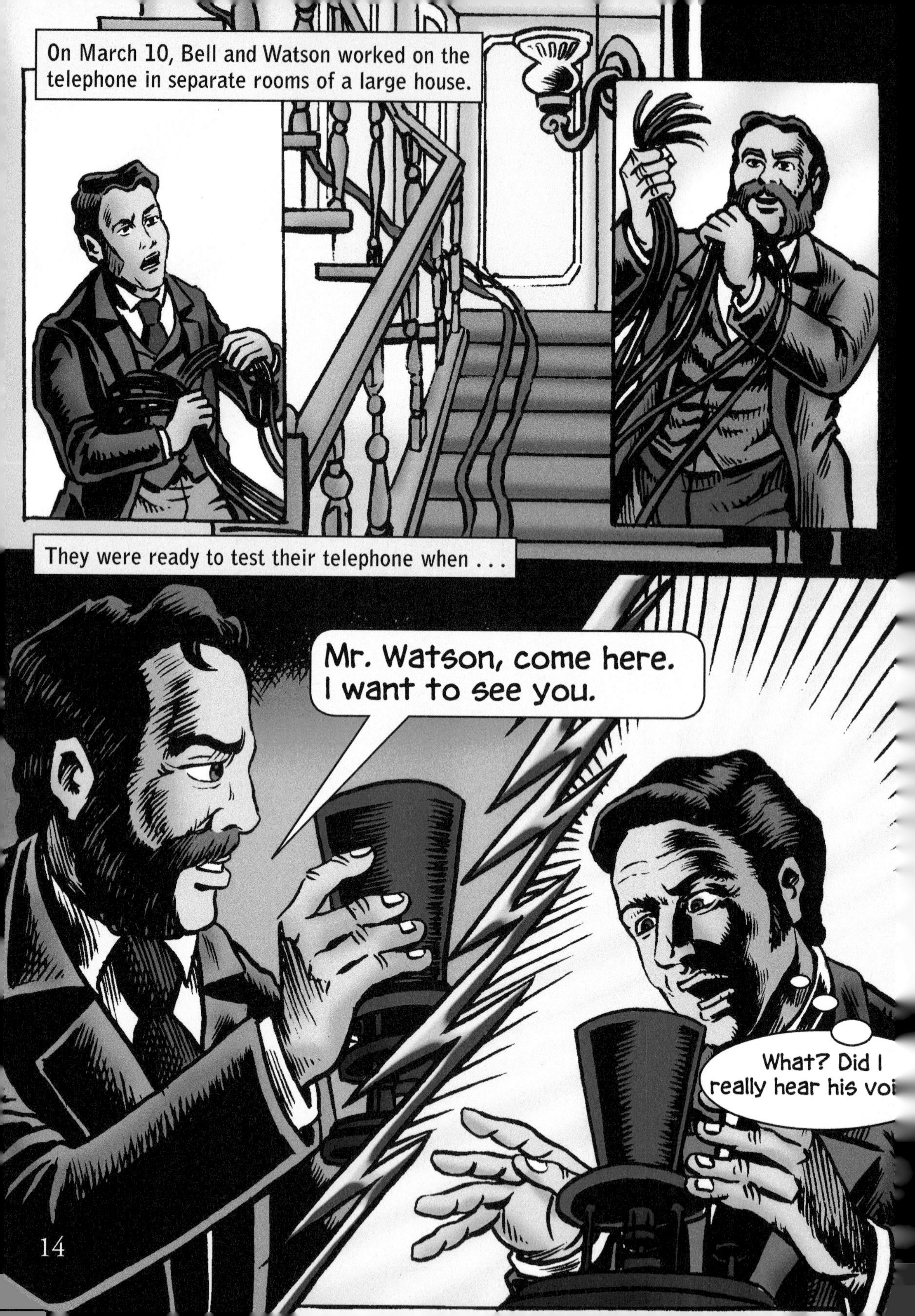
On March 10, Bell and Watson worked on the telephone in separate rooms of a large house.
They were ready to test their telephone when . . .
Mr. Watson, come here. I want to see you.
What? Did I really hear his voi

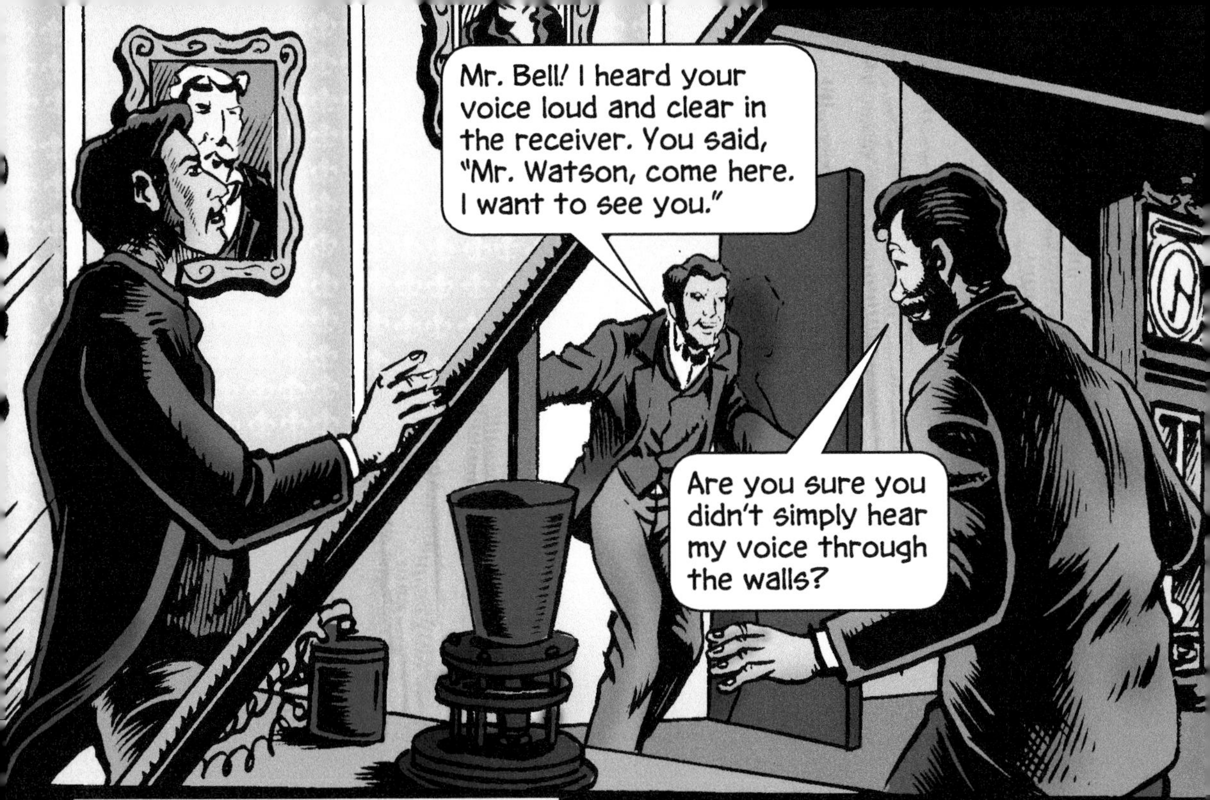
Mr. Bell! I heard your voice loud and clear in the receiver. You said, "Mr. Watson, come here. I want to see you."
Are you sure you didn't simply hear my voice through the walls?

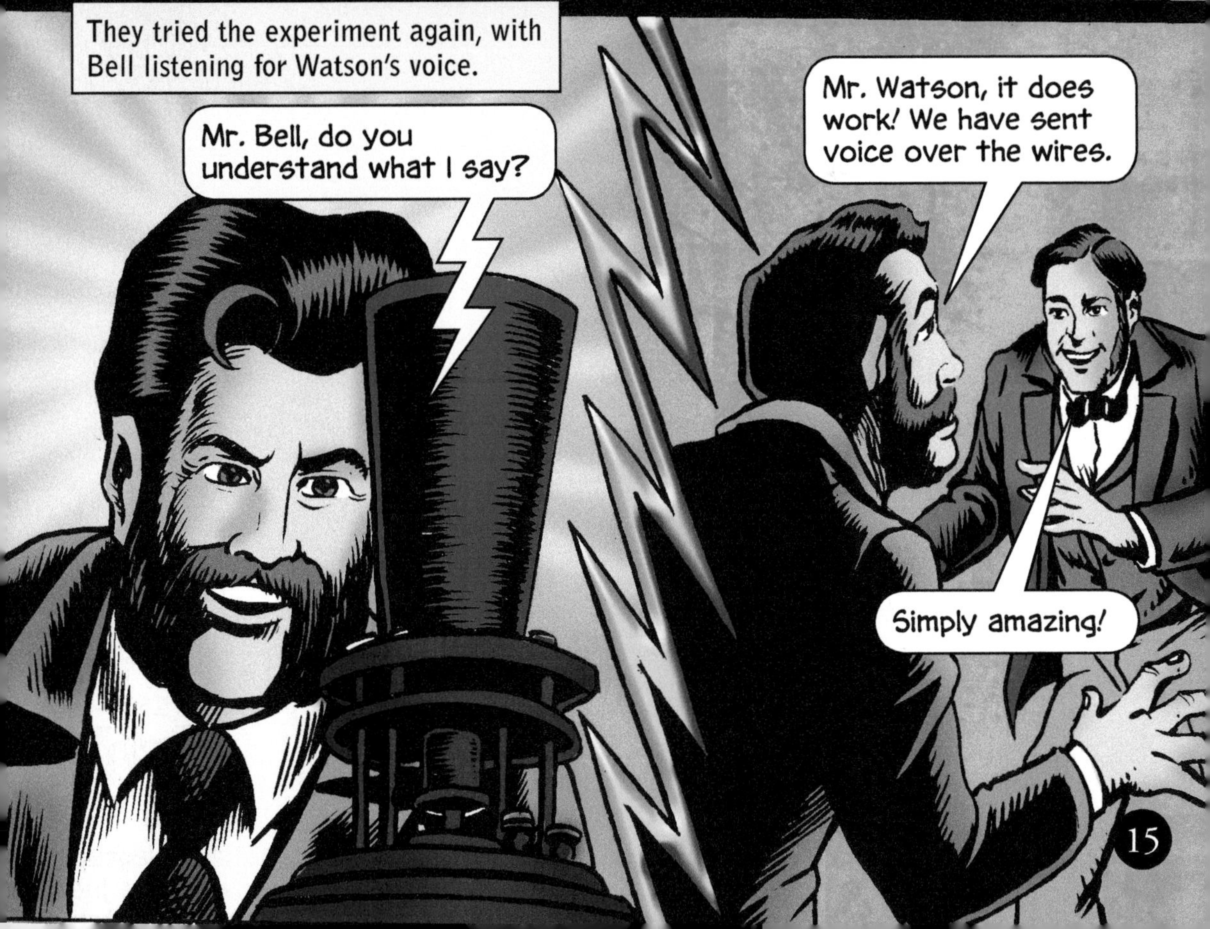
They tried the experiment again, with Bell listening for Watson's voice.
Mr. Bell, do you understand what I say?
Mr. Watson, it does work! We have sent voice over the wires.
Simply amazing!

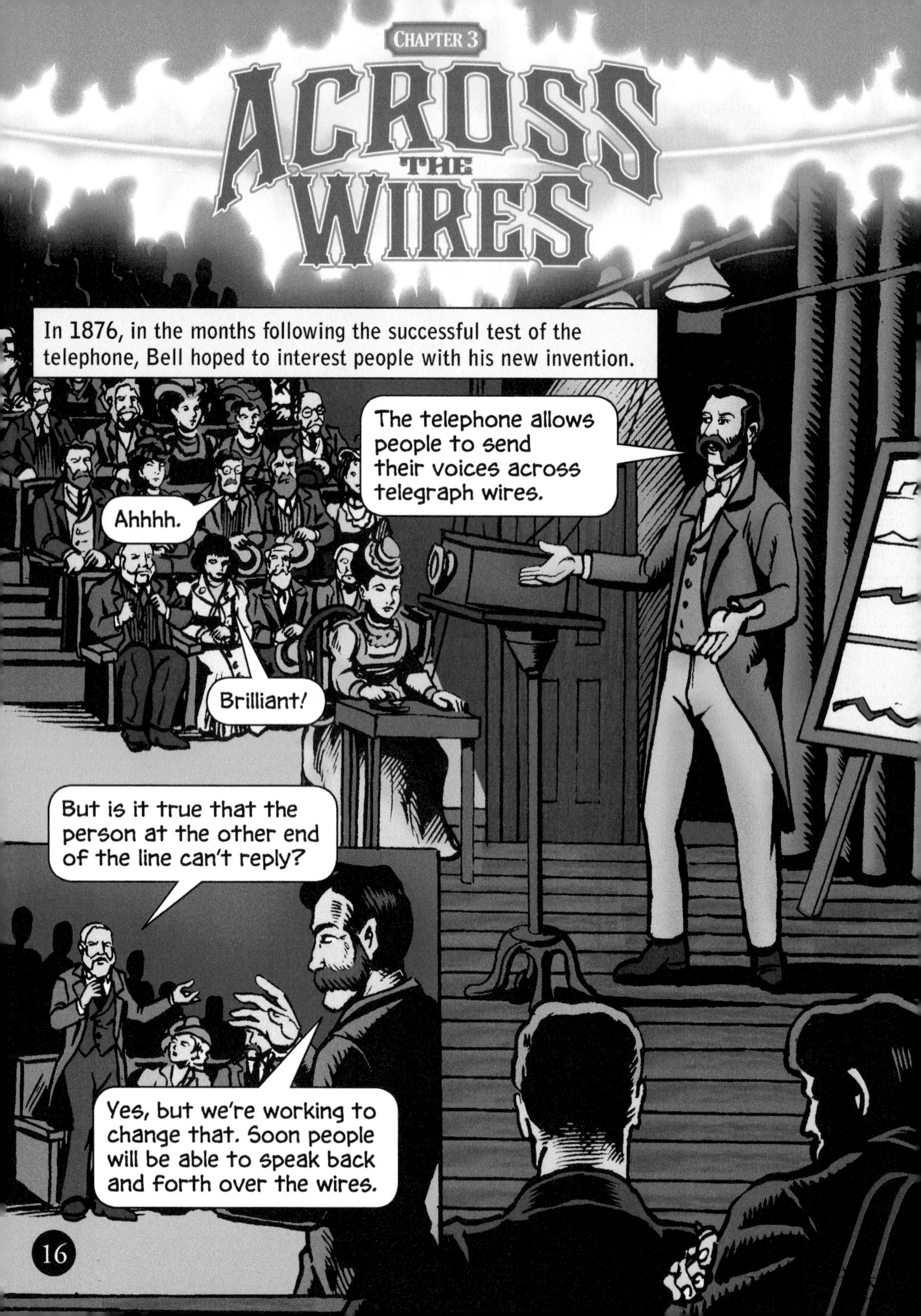
CHAPTER 3
ACROSS THE WIRES
In 1876, in the months following the successful test of the telephone, Bell hoped to interest people with his new invention.
The telephone allows people to send their voices across telegraph wires.
Ahhhh.
Brilliant!
But is it true that the person at the other end of the line can't reply?
Yes, but we're working to change that. Soon people will be able to speak back and forth over the wires.

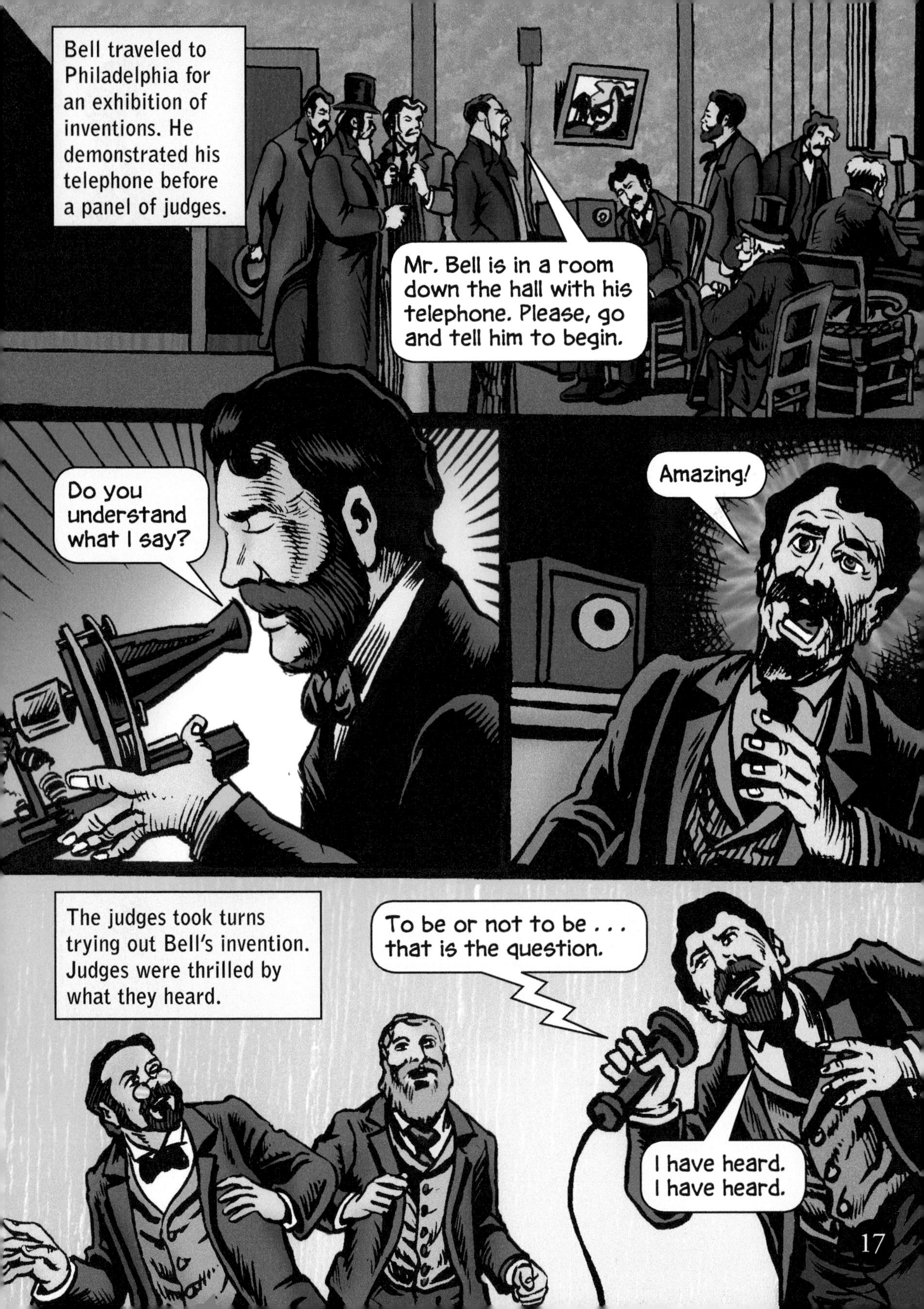

Bell traveled to Philadelphia for an exhibition of inventions. He demonstrated his telephone before a panel of judges.
Mr. Bell is in a room down the hall with his telephone. Please, go and tell him to begin.
Do you understand what I say?
Amazing!
The judges took turns trying out Bell's invention. Judges were thrilled by what they heard.
To be or not to be . . . that is the question.
I have heard. I have heard.

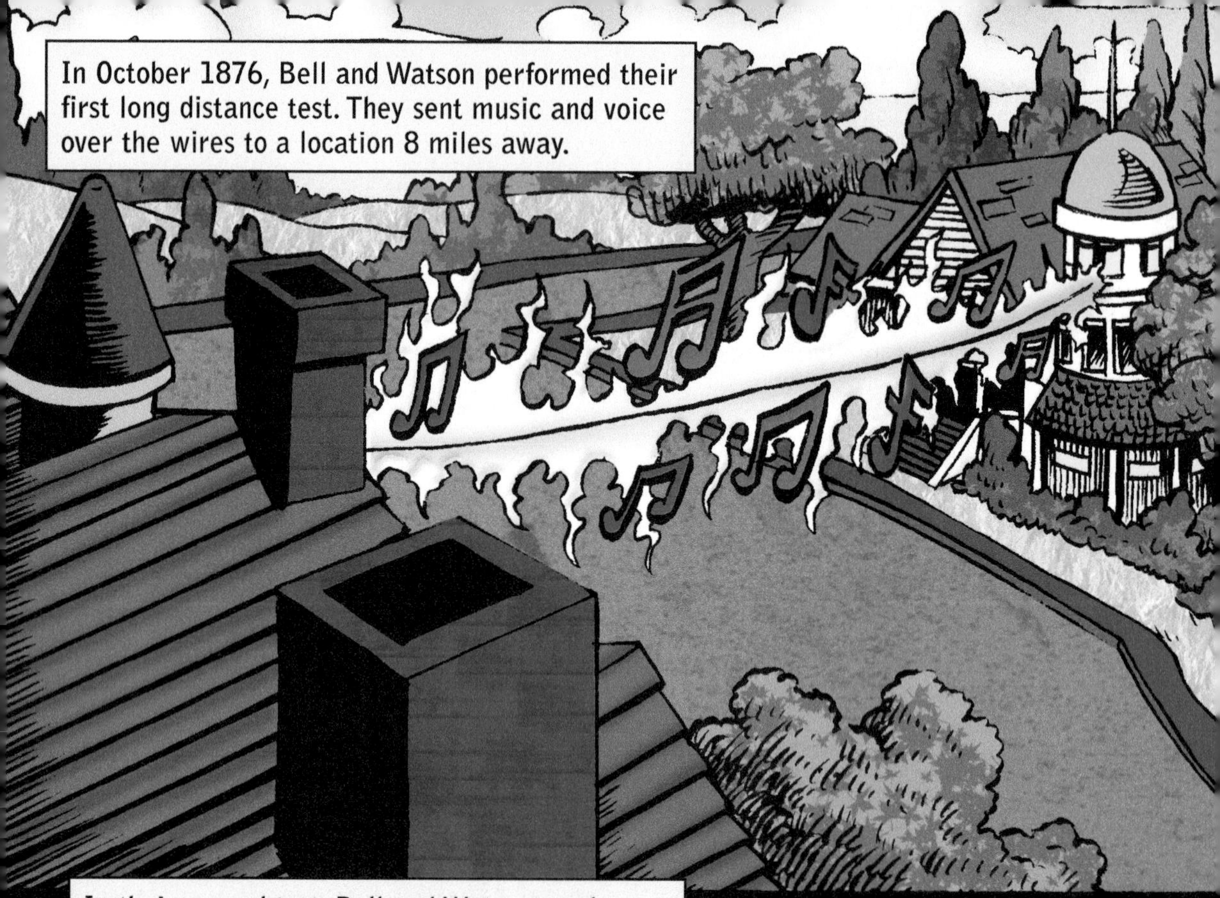
In October 1876, Bell and Watson performed their first long distance test. They sent music and voice over the wires to a location 8 miles away.

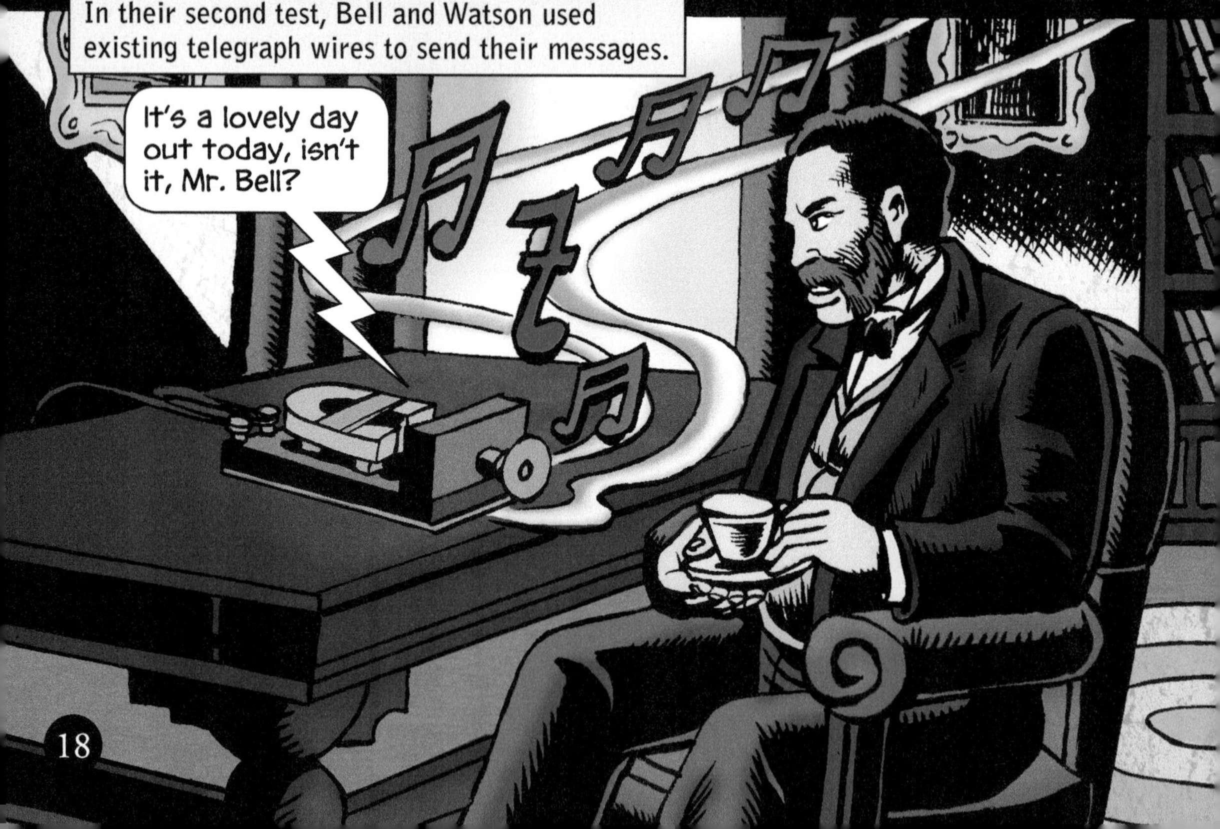
In their second test, Bell and Watson used existing telegraph wires to send their messages.
It's a lovely day out today, isn't it, Mr. Bell?

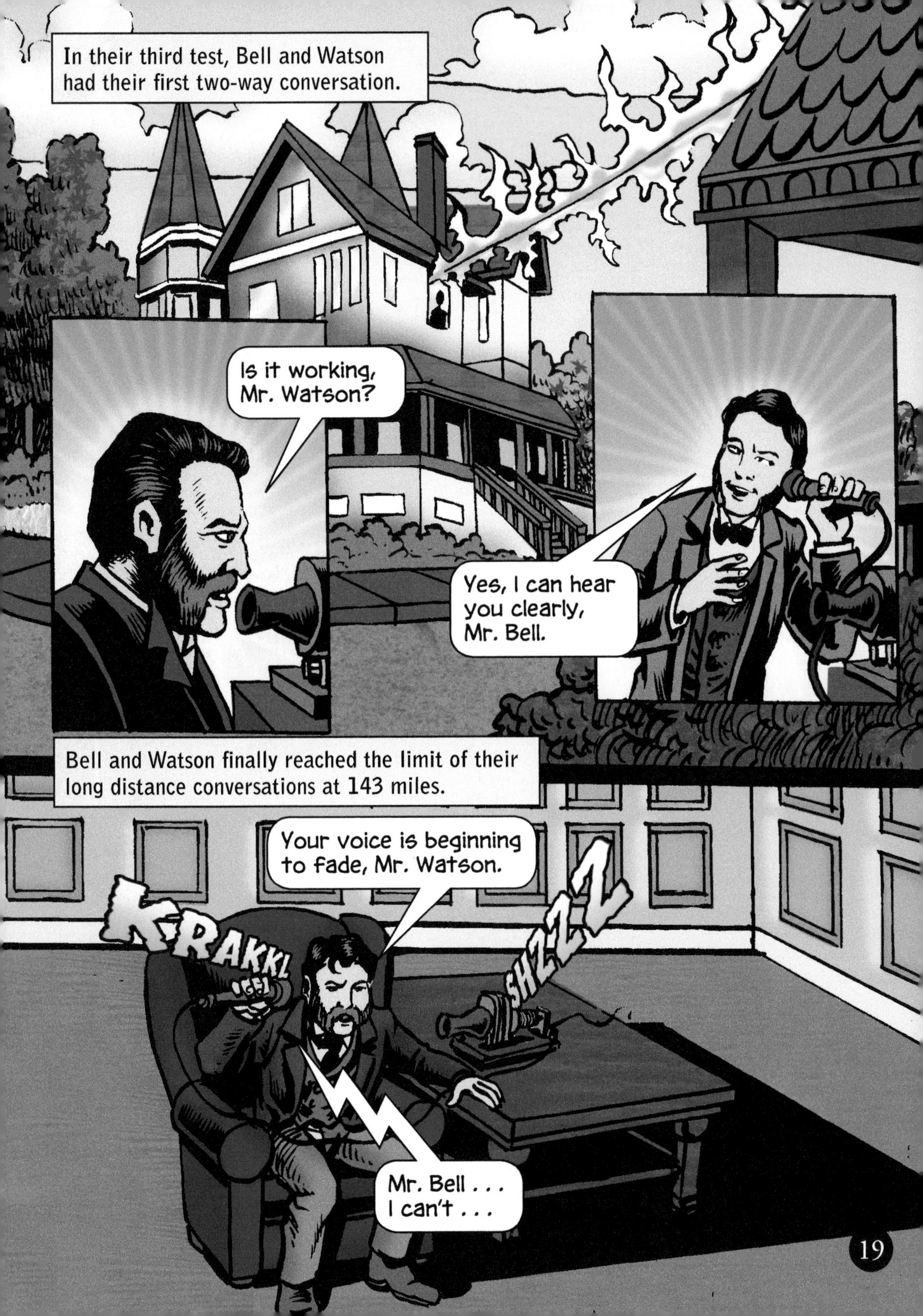

In their third test, Bell and Watson had their first two-way conversation.
Is it working, Mr. Watson?
Yes, I can hear you clearly, Mr. Bell.
Bell and Watson finally reached the limit of their long distance conversations at 143 miles.
Your voice is beginning to fade, Mr. Watson.
KRAKKL
SHZZZ
Mr. Bell . . . I can't . . .

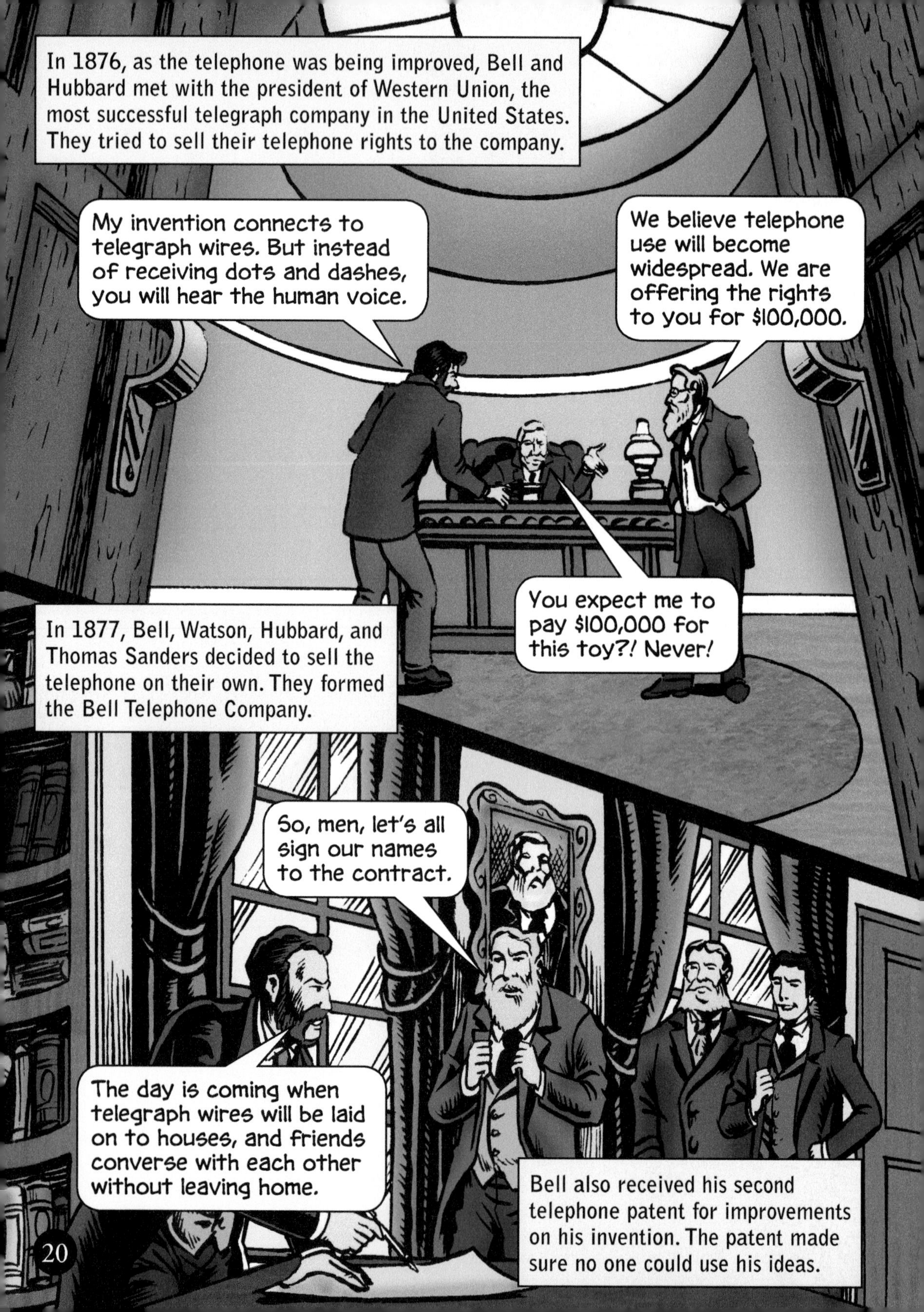
In 1876, as the telephone was being improved, Bell and Hubbard met with the president of Western Union, the most successful telegraph company in the United States. They tried to sell their telephone rights to the company.
My invention connects to telegraph wires. But instead of receiving dots and dashes, you will hear the human voice.
We believe telephone use will become widespread. We are offering the rights to you for $100,000.
You expect me to pay $100,000 for this toy?! Never!
In 1877, Bell, Watson, Hubbard, and Thomas Sanders decided to sell the telephone on their own. They formed the Bell Telephone Company.
So, men, let's all sign our names to the contract.
The day is coming when telegraph wires will be laid on to houses, and friends converse with each other without leaving home.
Bell also received his second telephone patent for improvements on his invention. The patent made sure no one could use his ideas.

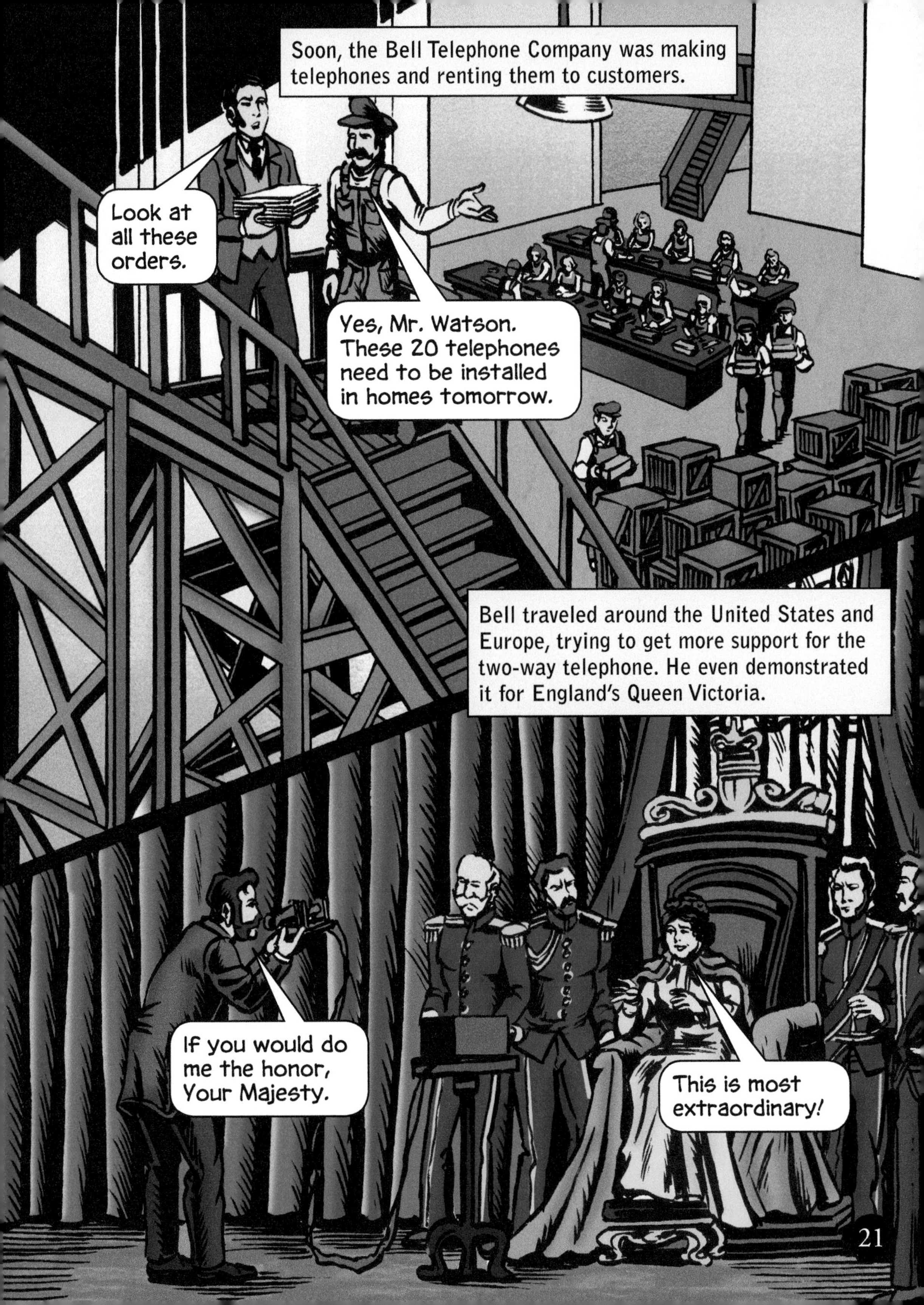
Soon, the Bell Telephone Company was making telephones and renting them to customers.
Look at all these orders.
Yes, Mr. Watson. These 20 telephones need to be installed in homes tomorrow.
Bell traveled around the United States and Europe, trying to get more support for the two-way telephone. He even demonstrated it for England's Queen Victoria.
If you would do me the honor, Your Majesty.
This is most extraordinary!

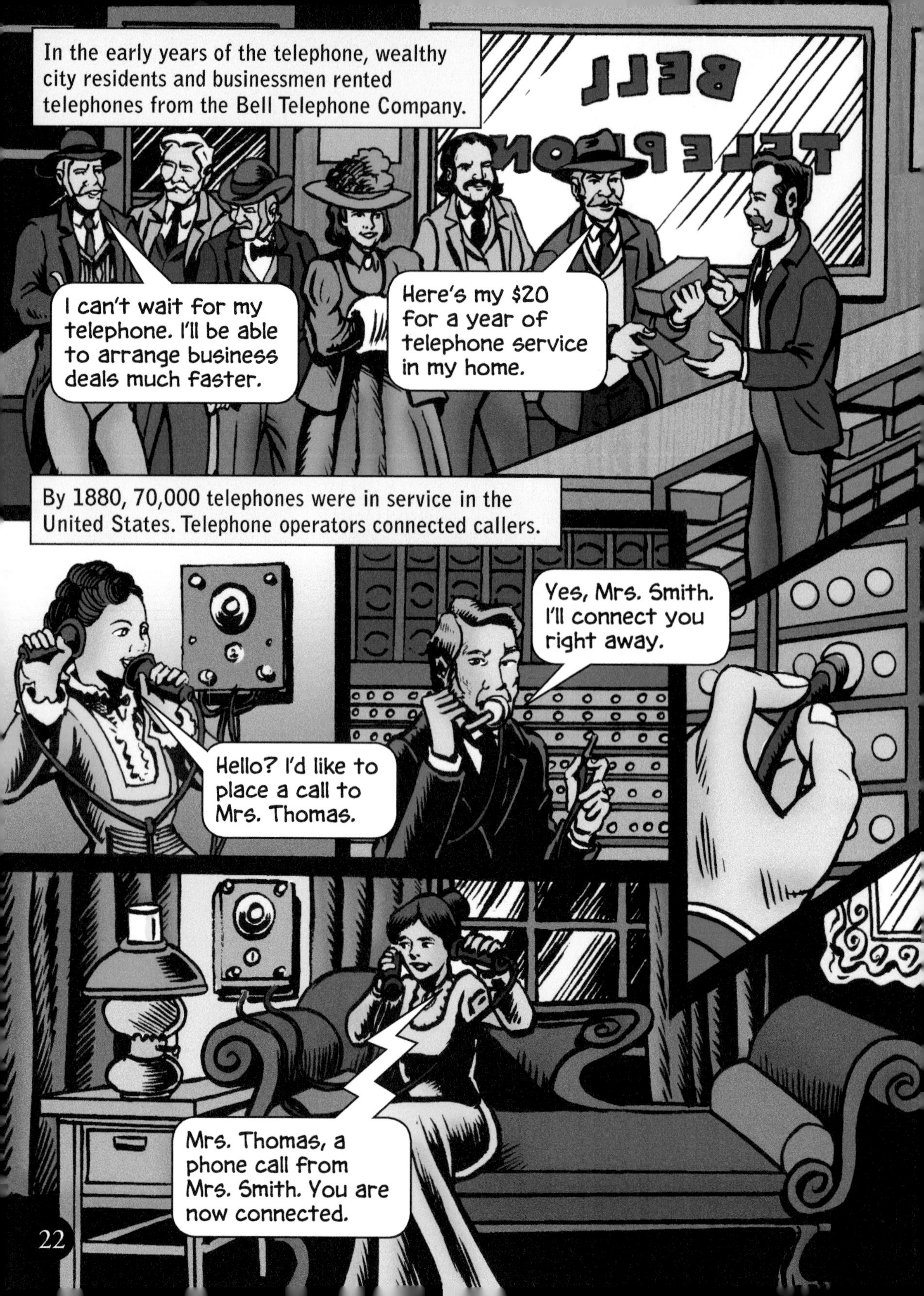
In the early years of the telephone, wealthy city residents and businessmen rented telephones from the Bell Telephone Company.
I can't wait for my telephone. I'll be able to arrange business deals much faster.
Here's my $20 for a year of telephone service in my home.
By 1880, 70,000 telephones were in service in the United States. Telephone operators connected callers.
Hello? I'd like to place a call to Mrs. Thomas.
Yes, Mrs. Smith. I'll connect you right away.
Mrs. Thomas, a phone call from Mrs. Smith. You are now connected.

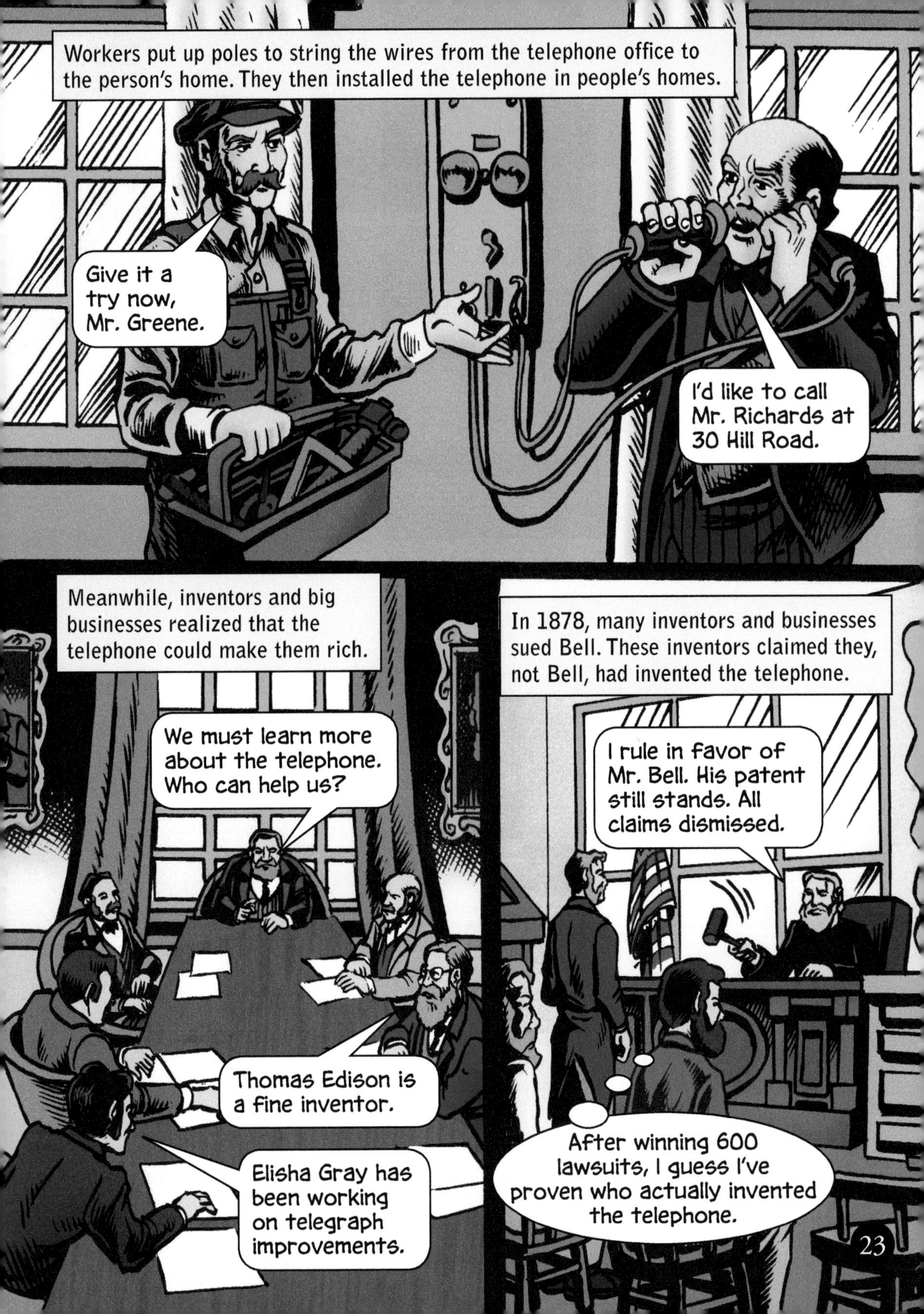
Workers put up poles to string the wires from the telephone office to the person's home. They then installed the telephone in people's homes.
Give it a try now, Mr. Greene.
I'd like to call Mr. Richards at 30 Hill Road.
Meanwhile, inventors and big businesses realized that the telephone could make them rich.
We must learn more about the telephone. Who can help us?
Thomas Edison is a fine inventor.
Elisha Gray has been working on telegraph improvements.
In 1878, many inventors and businesses sued Bell. These inventors claimed they, not Bell, had invented the telephone.
I rule in favor of Mr. Bell. His patent still stands. All claims dismissed.
After winning 600 lawsuits, I guess I've proven who actually invented the telephone.

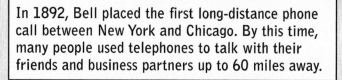

CHAPTER 4

CONNECTING THE WORLD

In 1892, Bell placed the first long-distance phone call between New York and Chicago. By this time, many people used telephones to talk with their friends and business partners up to 60 miles away.

Hoy, Hoy, Mr. Watson. Are you there?

Yes, Mr. Bell. I can hear you loud and clear.

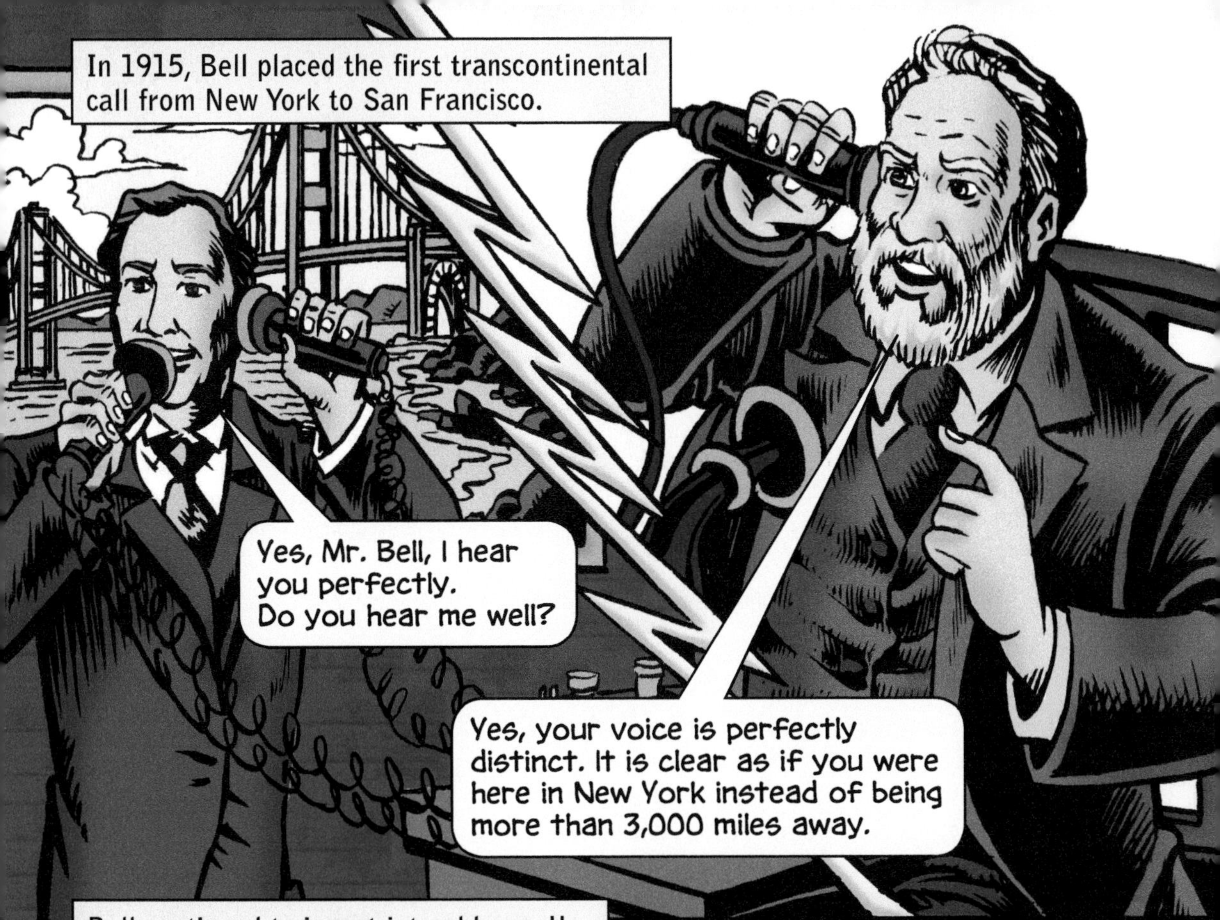
In 1915, Bell placed the first transcontinental call from New York to San Francisco.
Yes, Mr. Bell, I hear you perfectly. Do you hear me well?
Yes, your voice is perfectly distinct. It is clear as if you were here in New York instead of being more than 3,000 miles away.

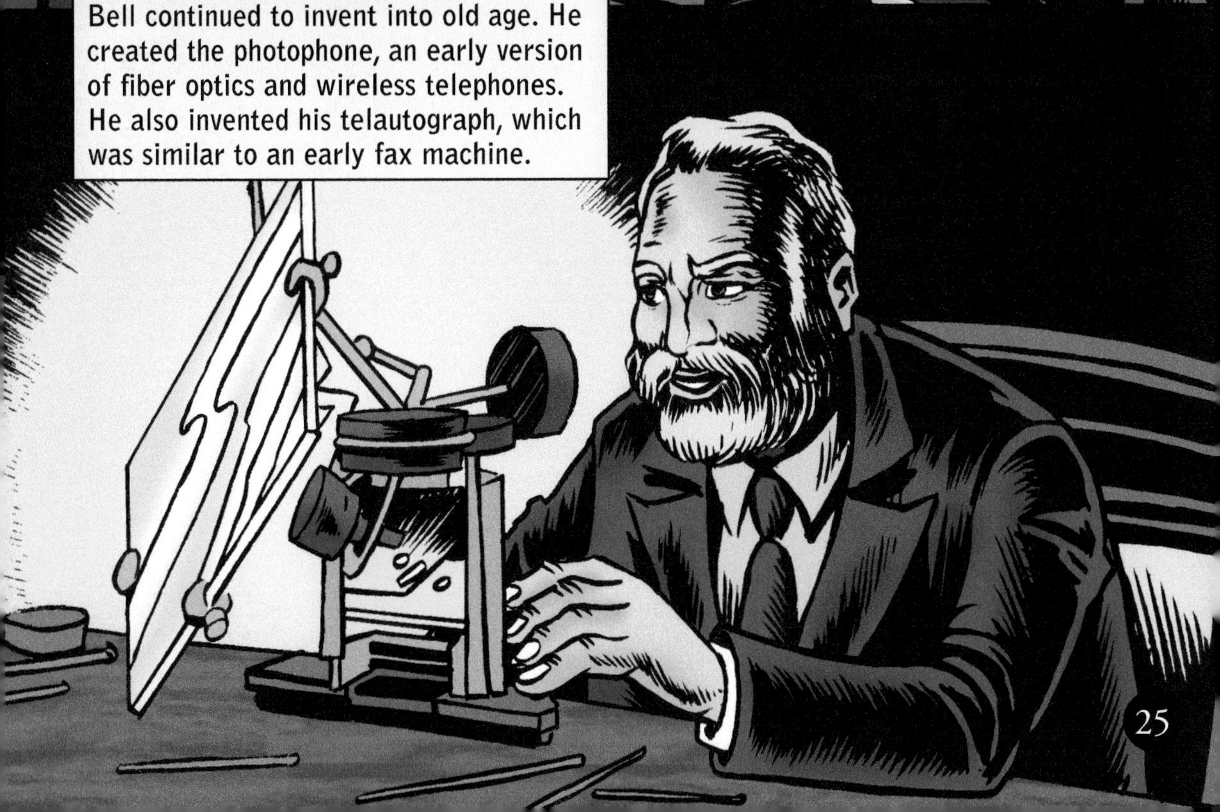
Bell continued to invent into old age. He created the photophone, an early version of fiber optics and wireless telephones. He also invented his telautograph, which was similar to an early fax machine.

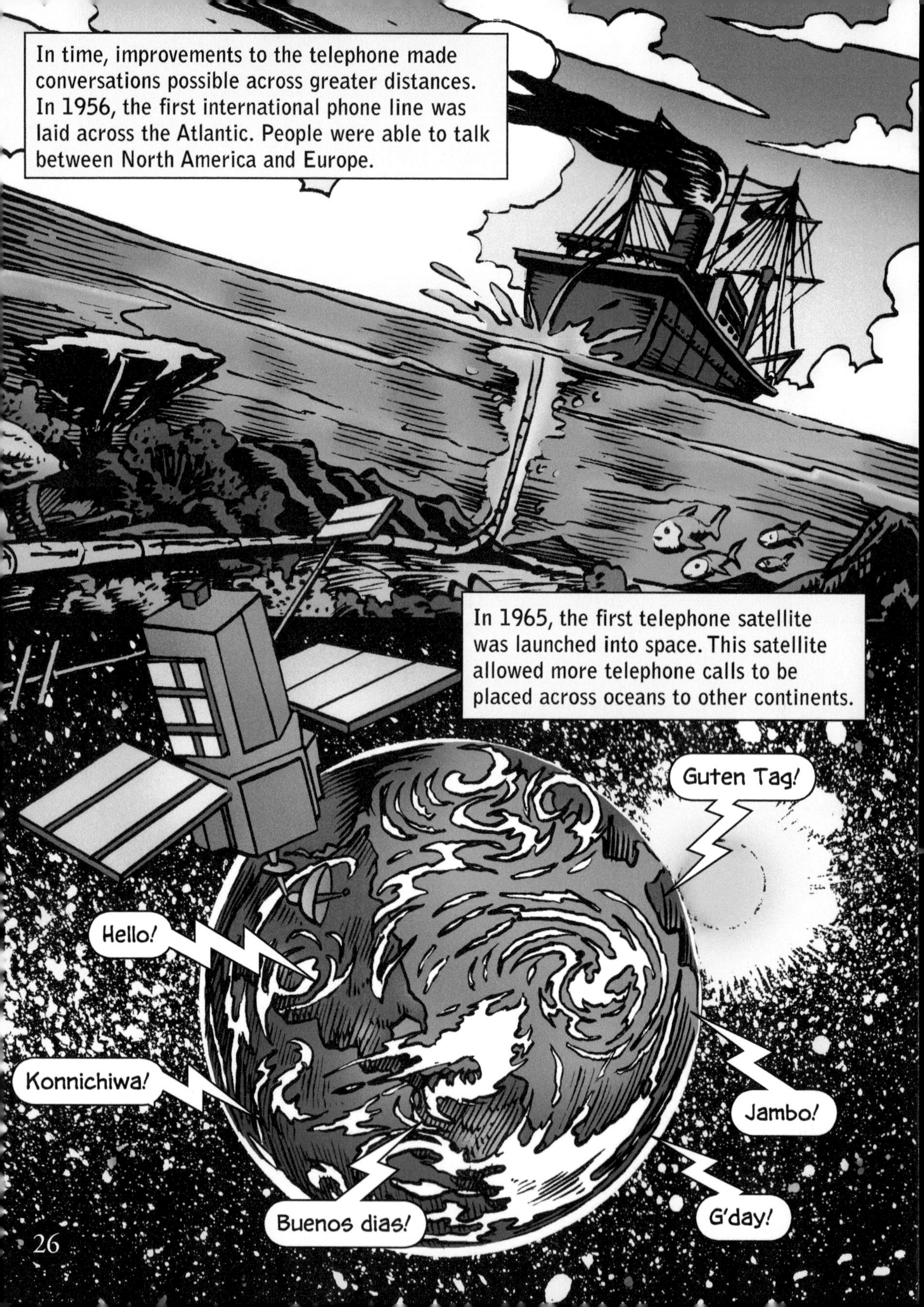
In time, improvements to the telephone made conversations possible across greater distances. In 1956, the first international phone line was laid across the Atlantic. People were able to talk between North America and Europe.
In 1965, the first telephone satellite was launched into space. This satellite allowed more telephone calls to be placed across oceans to other continents.
Guten Tag!
Hello!
Konnichiwa!
Jambo!
Buenos dias!
G'day!

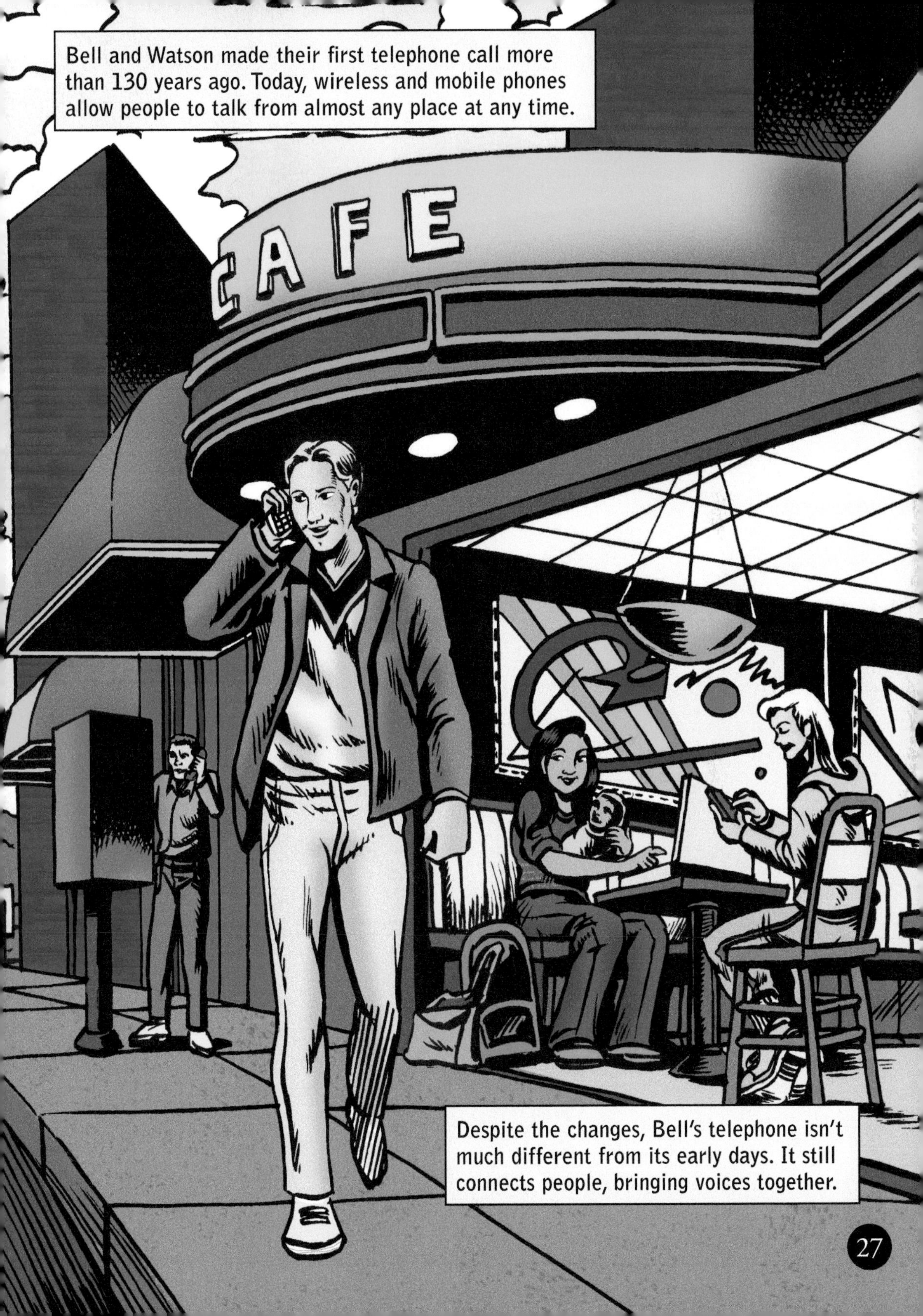
Bell and Watson made their first telephone call more than 130 years ago. Today, wireless and mobile phones allow people to talk from almost any place at any time.
CAFE
Despite the changes, Bell's telephone isn't much different from its early days. It still connects people, bringing voices together.

MORE ABOUT BELL AND THE TELEPHONE

Alexander Graham Bell was born March 3, 1847, in Edinburgh, Scotland. He died at his home in Canada on August 2, 1922.

Bell believed his understanding of sound led him to create the first telephone. His father was an elocutionist, a person who teaches proper speech. He encouraged his sons to understand how the human voice works.

As teenagers, Bell and his brothers studied the human body and created a "speaking machine." They molded the mouth, tongue, throat, and lungs out of wax. When they forced air into the machine, they moved the mouth to form different words.

Bell worked as a teacher of elocution and music in his late teenage years. In his 20s, he worked as a teacher of the deaf, first in London, and then in the United States. Bell believed that deaf people should read lips and learn speech to communicate, instead of using sign language.

Bell married Mabel Hubbard, the daughter of Gardiner Greene Hubbard, in 1877. Mabel was deaf, and had been a student of Bell's.

- The invention of the telephone has been debated since Bell received his first patent in 1876. In the 1850s, Italian immigrant Antonio Meucci began work on a talking telegraph. He filed paperwork for his idea in the U.S. patent office, but he never received a patent. Also, in the 1860s, a German schoolteacher named Philipp Reis invented a device that sent sounds electronically over wires. He tried to send voice over the wires, but there were problems with his device.

- The decibel, the unit for measuring sound, is named after Bell.

- In 1922, on the day of Alexander Graham Bell's funeral, all telephones in North America went silent for one minute to honor his life and his invention.

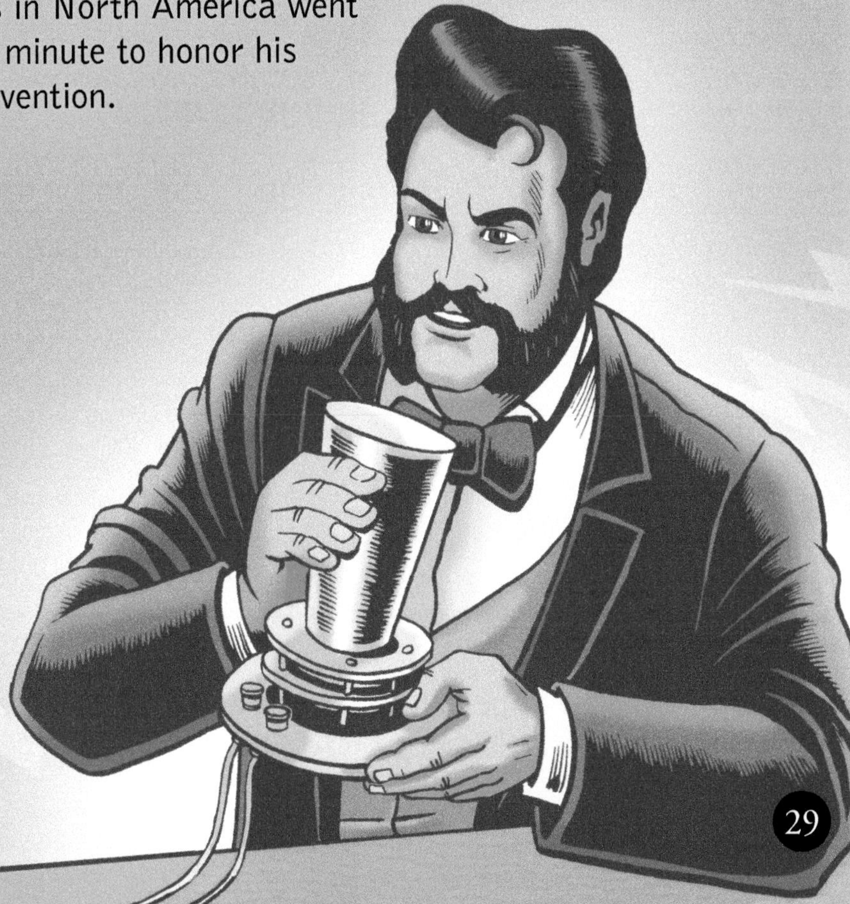

GLOSSARY

harmonic (har-MON-ik)—a way to describe different sounds played at the same time

patent (PAT-uhnt)—a legal document that gives an inventor the right to make, use, or sell an invention for a set period of years

pitch (PICH)—the highness or lowness of a sound; vibrations change a sound's pitch.

satellite (SAT-uh-lite)—a spacecraft that circles the earth; satellites gather and send information.

transcontinental (transs-kon-tuh-NEN-tuhl)—extending or going across a continent

vibration (vye-BRA-shuhn)—a fast movement back and forth; vibrations in the throat are caused by air from the lungs.

INTERNET SITES

FactHound offers a safe, fun way to find Internet sites related to this book. All of the sites on FactHound have been researched by our staff.

Here's how:

1. Visit *www.facthound.com*
2. Choose your grade level.
3. Type in this book ID **0736864784** for age-appropriate sites. You may also browse subjects by clicking on letters, or by clicking on pictures and words.
4. Click on the **Fetch It** button.

FactHound will fetch the best sites for you!

Read More

Bankston, John. *Alexander Graham Bell and the Story of the Telephone.* Uncharted, Unexplored, and Unexplained. Hockessin, Del.: Mitchell Lane, 2005.

Durrett, Deanne. *Alexander Graham Bell.* Inventors and Creators. San Diego: KidHaven Press, 2003.

Jarnow, Jesse. *Telegraph and Telephone Networks: Groundbreaking Developments in American Communication.* America's Industrial Society in the 19th Century. New York: Rosen, 2004.

Nobleman, Marc Tyler. *The Telephone.* Great Inventions. Mankato, Minn.: Capstone Press, 2004.

Bibliography

Alexander Graham Bell Family Papers at the Library of Congress
http://memory.loc.gov/ammem/bellhtml/bellhome.html

Bruce, Robert V. *Bell: Alexander Graham Bell and the Conquest of Solitude.* Boston: Little, Brown, 1973.

Grosvenor, Edwin S., and Morgan Wesson. *Alexander Graham Bell: The Life and Times of the Man Who Invented the Telephone.* New York: Harry Abrams, 1997.

INDEX